Back
to the
Prairie

Back
to the
Prairie

A Home Remade, A Life Rediscovered

MELISSA GILBERT

G

GALLERY BOOKS

New York   London   Toronto   Sydney   New Delhi

G

Gallery Books
An Imprint of Simon & Schuster, Inc.
1230 Avenue of the Americas
New York, NY 10020

First Gallery Books trade paperback edition June 2023

GALLERY BOOKS and colophon are registered trademarks of Simon & Schuster, Inc.

For information about special discounts for bulk purchases, please contact Simon & Schuster Special Sales at 1-866-506-1949 or business@simonandschuster.com.

The Simon & Schuster Speakers Bureau can bring authors to your live event. For more information or to book an event, contact the Simon & Schuster Speakers Bureau at 1-866-248-3049 or visit our website at www.simonspeakers.com.

Interior design by Davina Mock-Maniscalco

Manufactured in the United States of America

10 9 8 7 6 5 4 3 2 1

Library of Congress Control Number: 2021952266

ISBN 978-1-9821-7718-8
ISBN 978-1-9821-7719-5 (pbk)
ISBN 978-1-9821-7720-1 (ebook)

*For my sweet, perfect grandchildren who have filled
this second half of my life with immeasurable joy.
I love you each to the moon and back.*

And now here is my secret, a very simple secret:
It is only with the heart that one can see rightly;
what is essential is invisible to the eye.

THE LITTLE PRINCE

Contents

Back to the
to the
Prairie

Foreword

by Timothy Busfield

There are many people who could write a foreword to this book: those who read the book and then weigh in; those who know the author and then weigh in on what they have read; and those who read the book, know the author, and were there to validate its truth. I am the only one who fits the latter. I was there for all of it.

I don't like to read books. I often joke that the last book I read was the Yogi Berra story in ninth grade, but that's not really true. I read for a living. I read scripts. I am always reading a script for a project I am preparing to either act in or direct, or scripts that others have sent to me asking for feedback. I also read the news. What I can't seem to do is commit to a book, because something will inevitably pull me off it and I may not return. I've started every novel Michael Crichton ever wrote but finished only three of them. But I wanted to read *this* book all the way through for a personal reason: I didn't trust my wife to get the facts right. However, I have now read this book, and I can tell you that I have no quibbles. The story is one hundred percent correct.

Melissa Gilbert is my wife. She is exactly the way her fans imagine her to be: kind, sweet, determined, funny, and a champion in the charity of forgiveness. They think of her as a grown-up Laura Ingalls Wilder, the character she played throughout her childhood on the classic TV show *Little House on the Prairie*, and if you're talking about her heart and soul, wisdom and humanity, and eagerness to learn, they aren't wrong. But she was not raised a country girl—she doesn't have an iota of prairie in her. She's a Jewish girl from Encino, California, and as a child, the closest she came to picking vegetables from a garden was when she went to Gelson's market to get a tomato for her bagel.

When Melissa and I met, I was directing a television pilot in Los Angeles but lived full-time on a lake in Michigan. Melissa lived in a house in Studio City. She drove a convertible, her hair was fiery red, and her movie-star sunglasses were perfect. There was absolutely no anonymity to her life. When we were out, I'd hear the brakes on passing cars screech as people rubbernecked to see the beautiful icon I was sitting next to. She'd recently come off *Dancing with the Stars* and was fit, a perfect ten, and yet she was utterly confused about how to stay on the hamster wheel of Hollywood. She frequented her Botox specialist as if the doctor's office were a Starbucks drive-through. She was injected, augmented, and veneered, and doing everything right for an actress closing in on fifty trying to maintain a career as an ingénue.

When actresses hit middle age, they are no longer ingénues, period. They survive Hollywood's merciless insatiable appetite for youth because they embrace the character that time and experience adds to their face. They become character actresses. They evolve to stay in the game, and they stay in the game because they look evolved. It's the prize of age. I came into Melissa's life when she was at that midlife crossroads, deciding whether to hang on to the past or evolve to the next phase of her life and career, building on who she had been and who she wanted to be.

Melissa's whole life has been about adaptation, growth, and evolution. Born into a creative, blue-collar desert family in Nevada, she was put up for adoption the very day she arrived in this world. A glamorous, multigenerationally renowned Hollywood family claimed her as their own, raised her as a showbiz Valley girl, and loved her to pieces, as did millions of others who knew her as Laura Ingalls Wilder. In that role, she acted as though she loved animals and we believed her (because she really does). She made us think she rose early to milk cows (maybe not so much). She made us believe her values were rooted in family and the virtue of hard work, even if it meant breaking a fingernail (bingo!).

After Melissa and I found each other, we discovered that we were both craving a life away from the lights and pressures of Hollywood. I had moved to Michigan in early 2012, and after we married a year later, she packed up her bags and joined me in the slow lane of the Midwest. From the moment she left Detroit Metro Airport and found herself in the Michigan countryside, she melted into her natural self. After a few years of Great Lakes, snowstorms, and spring flowers, we moved to New York City for work. On the way, we stayed overnight in the Catskills. She was infatuated.

In 2019, we found property there and, in upstate New York, Melissa began her next—and current—chapter. She traded her Rodeo Drive wardrobe for overalls. Her bright red hair returned to its roots, literally. Her face moved again: Her forehead was freed from captivity, and I could tell when she questioned something. I watched her shed the years of playing the Hollywood game of vanity and self-promotion as Melissa Gilbert the star and become Melissa Gilbert the woman—the natural woman. This life wasn't just a more relaxed fit. It was a natural fit.

"Fireflies!" she'd shriek joyously. "Baby deer!" she'd call out. She became a DIY guru. She raised chickens. She tended our garden. She was at home—and she was *home*. I was the yuppie guy from *thirtysomething* and Poindexter from the *Nerds* movies. I was unable to put a table saw together. But Melissa could, and did. I don't know if this could have happened had we not experienced the COVID-19 pandemic and found ourselves in a time and place where normal no longer applied. I want to believe it would have. If you're open, if you ask the right questions, you find yourself. If you're lucky, you find someone who makes you find your best self. I am lucky.

As I look at her while writing the introduction to this book, which is about all of the above, I see a natural beauty. The most natural beauty. This book will help you see the transition from what she felt people wanted her to be, and what she thought she needed to be, to the amazing person she knew she was and is. This book is a true story. And I can tell you that she got the facts right. It's been so fun for us to grow in this direction, like the sunflower that bends to the light as it shoots skyward and explodes into a burst of bright yellow florets and petals. I witnessed this story she has told here and have relished the chance to grow and bloom alongside her. It's been quite an experience, a gentle unfolding of a remarkable life that, even more remarkably, you will find relatable and hopefully encouraging of the many possibilities life can hold. I envy this woman; she inspires me every day. And I love being Melissa Gilbert's husband. She is my beloved.

Enjoy this story from my extraordinary wife, and a beautiful soul. Maybe let it help you see that it's never too late to find your natural self . . . brave change, open your heart, and evolve.

Part One

Home is the nicest word there is.

LAURA INGALLS WILDER,

FROM NBC'S *LITTLE HOUSE ON THE PRAIRIE*

Escape from New York

Tim found the house on Zillow in early fall 2019, though calling the structure he saw a house is generous.

He was scrolling through properties in upstate New York. The Catskills, to be specific. We were living in New York City and wanted a second home where we could escape into peace, quiet, and nature. We wanted space to think and breathe and stillness to help us slow down. We wanted to recharge and feel inspired. That kind of thinking led us to the . . . house.

Scrolling through Zillow is something I have done since I heard that other people do it to pass the time. Like them, I look at homes around the world. Castles, mansions, lake homes, oceanfront palaces, architectural gems, my childhood homes, tree houses, houseboats, and cool-looking structures that are served up randomly.

It's better than doomscrolling, which is about searching for and reading the endless flow of articles that confirm the world is screwed and so, by proxy, are we. Pick your poison. There are plenty out there. Global warming, pandemics, uncompromising politicians, the end of democracy, conspiracy theories. We didn't need to get into doomscrolling the way others did. We could turn on our favorite cable news network for all the news that was fit to panic over.

Admittedly, some of that life-is-getting-out-of-control mindset did contribute to our desire to find a place outside of the city. Not too far, though. We didn't want to be more than two or three hours away by car in case one or both of us had to work, cracked a tooth, or craved sushi. In that respect, we were kind of like kids learning to ride a two-wheeler bike, yelling at their parents, "Don't let go! Don't let go!" Then, suddenly, and without realizing, we were pedaling on our own in the country with gardens, chickens, and bears, oh my!

That's kind of the whole story in a nutshell—but not really.

The story encompasses divorce, bloodshed, Botox, an unhealthy relationship, love, pulling up roots, marriage—or I should say remarriage—blended families, snakes, rodents, growing food, roosters and hens, power tools, generators, a pandemic, wild animals, and survival, among other things. Some might say this is about a midlife crisis. I call it a midlife reassessment of priorities and my realization that real satisfaction and meaning, for me, at fifty-six years old, came from canning tomatoes and cleaning the chicken coop rather than implants and hair color and other efforts to stop time from marching across my face.

The word that comes to mind is *simplification*.

I'm not sure getting to the point where I am now was always simple. But maybe it was. Maybe it was inevitable. Maybe the decisions we make, even the bad ones, are bread crumbs on the path we're supposed to follow. Maybe I was destined to hear my husband, the actor, director, and shoulder-rubber extraordinaire Timothy Busfield, look up from the Zillow listing on his computer screen and say, "I think we should investigate this place."

At that point, Tim and I, as a couple, were relative newcomers to New York, though we had both lived there for various stretches over the years. Married for five years, we had begun our legal life together in Michigan but transplanted ourselves to Manhattan after numerous conversations that went like this:

Tim: Where do you want to go for dinner tonight?
Me: New York.

Me: What do you want to do this weekend?
Tim: Go to New York.

Tim: Should we go to the movies tonight?
Me: Sure. What's playing in New York?

So we went to New York, a fine place for two people in our line of work, though, after four years in Michigan's slow lane, we weren't sure that we wanted to stay. To underscore the point, we moved into an Airbnb in Harlem. It was the lowest-level commitment available. No first month's rent, last month's rent, security deposit, broker's fee, bribes to the building's board. In other words, none of the usual welcome-to–New York expenditures. It was like we were visiting. And almost immediately I was cast in a play. When that ended, I got another play. The message was as clear as my name was on the theater marquee. We decided to stay.

We found an apartment on the Upper West Side, which turned out to be too noisy. I actually listed our upstairs neighbors' phone number in my contacts as "Stompers." From there, we moved to a smaller one-bedroom, one-bath in a great building that's in an equally great location, where we still rent. It's a block and a half from the train station at Seventy-Second, which was convenient when I had to get to the theater, or anywhere, for that matter. The building is seven stories, with only four apartments on each floor, so we don't have a ton of neighbors. They may say the same about us: *We don't have a ton of Melissa and Tim.*

Both of us did well in the city. I had my theater routine and Tim was directing and acting on a variety of TV shows, including *Law & Order: SVU*. We were busy, and our friends and family kept us busier. One of our favorite things to do was to send out a group text saying that we were going to the five o'clock showing of whatever movie, and everybody, including Tim's son Willy and my son Michael, both of whom had recently moved to New York, would meet at the theater, and we would go out to dinner en masse afterward. We had several groups of people and hung out all the time. We also went to the theater and the museums. We were a fifty-something and a sixtysomething hanging out with twenty- and thirtysomethings along with folks our own age.

It was very fun, but even in the best of circumstances the city closes in on you. There is always someone on the other side of the wall, up above, or down below. Sidewalks are crowded, subway cars can feel more like stuffy petri dishes for cultivating odd spores and germs, and everything is kind of dirty and difficult. Not that we mind or complain. Tim and I chose life in the Big Apple. We hearted

New York—the good, the bad, and the parts that occasionally made us feel like we were lucky to escape with our lives.

But living there can get intense and claustrophobic, and . . . and loud. I have hypersensitive hearing. Actually, I have misophonia, a condition that causes certain sounds to drive me absolutely insane. Like chewing sounds, the crunching of popcorn or tortilla chips, a certain frequency of television sound coming through the wall, or the droning of voices in that same tone.

Sirens, barking dogs, vacuum cleaners—they don't register. It's the weird stuff that makes me want to murder or run away. I'm a freak.

Tim can't hear too awfully well. He has hearing aids but never wears them because . . . because why would he want to listen to me complain about things that I hear?

But he does like to get outside in the fresh air.

And so it became important for us to have a place where we could escape.

"We need space," Tim said.

Back in Los Angeles, where I grew up, *space* meant a gleaming, white, five-thousand-square-foot Cape Cod–style farmhouse with a kitchen full of stainless steel appliances, including the de rigueur Wolf range, a media room, a wine cellar, a gym, a primary suite with a lavish spa-equivalent bathroom, a pool, an outdoor kitchen with a pizza oven, a massage pavilion, a tennis court, a dog-grooming station, and a two-bedroom guesthouse. Depending on the neighborhood, that kind of space could run anywhere between four and one hundred million dollars. In New York, *space* is shorthand for "let's get a place in the country," and *the country* is a euphemism for either "the Hamptons" or "upstate New York." Billionaires heli-copter out to Southampton, East Hampton, and Sag Harbor. Regu-lar old millionaires look at places in the Hudson Valley, Woodstock, Beacon, or even areas as far north as Lake Placid.

Then there are the renters, like us—and that's when Tim began scrolling on Zillow and I began aligning myself with reality. Be-cause when we first talked about looking for a country place, I was like anyone else. I dreamed big. I pictured a beautifully furnished vintage farmhouse with carefully curated grounds including rolling green fields, orchards, gardens, and woods, ready for its *Architec-tural Digest* photo shoot. It would have a pool, a bar, and a corral for the horses. It would be move-in ready. And then I woke up.

Fortunately, when I did wake up, it was in a cozy little place called the Stickett Inn. Tim and I had searched much farther up-state, but we ended up in Barryville, an adorable country refuge named after President Andrew Jackson's postmaster general, Wil-liam T. Barry, who—thank you, Wikipedia—was the only person in the cabinet not to resign as a result of the Petticoat Affair, which was essentially a scandal about a young woman who scared the shit out of the DC establishment by speaking her mind.

I liked her a lot—and I liked this funky place with the funny name. It was owned and operated by two guys, Roswell Hamrick and Johnny Pizzolato, a set designer and an actor/fashion guru; they lived in an old refurbished church behind the inn. The Stickett had four lovely, tastefully decorated guest rooms with fun names—Soak, Eat, Drink, and Steam. They also boasted a cabin called the Rear and a cozy bar/restaurant they named the Bang Bang Bar. Apparently their arrival in the area had irked some of the more small-minded folks there. What quicker way to ruin a two-hundred-year tradition of discrimination than letting two gay guys move in, right?

It was Johnny's mother who said, "Why don't you name the place Stickett Inn?" Which they did—and it stuck!

By the time we stayed there, Roswell had become president of the chamber of commerce and both of them were entrenched in the community. They took us under their wings, told us where to go for dinner, where to shop, and which towns to explore, and have consequently become our closest friends up here. We went up to the Stickett regularly, and that pocket of Sullivan County felt right. When we found our Realtor, Jill Steingart, we told her where we wanted to look and the kind of place we were looking for.

This was going to be the first home that Tim and I had owned together, and the financial reality, we explained, was nonnegotiable. We were going to have to do most of any work that needed to be done ourselves. If it was beyond our pay grade or dangerous, we would, of course, hire people. Otherwise, we were strictly DIY. Jill understood, and soon we made an offer on a tiny farmhouse in Barryville.

The first place we saw was a white clapboard farmhouse dating back to the 1800s, very Laura Ingalls Wilder's Rocky Ridge Farm, on multiple acres and next to a national forest, so no development would ever take place next to us. And the price was right—116,000 dollars.

It was supposed to be a short sale.

After months of radio silence, it turned out to be a no sale.

Jill took us around and showed us more places that she liked and we didn't. They were always *too*—too expensive, too together, or too new.

"You could bring people in with chains and they can age the wood paneling," she said. "You can make new look old."

I scratched my head.

"Why would I want to age a new house when I can restore an old one?" I said.

"We have to find the old one," she said.

"I think we already did," I said, and I gave her the details of the place Tim had found on Zillow.

From the pictures he showed me, I thought it looked interesting. That's a horribly nondescript word, a cop-out in most cases, but I meant it in the truest sense. I was interested. The place was somewhere between a house and a camp in the woods, a mishmash of styles with a stucco exterior and a shake roof. It was sort of cute. When I shuttled through the photos, I got the sense that it needed a hug as much as it did a remodel. The most attractive feature was the land. It was on fourteen wooded acres, and from what I could tell, the neighbors were far enough away that the place struck us as a hidden gem, a frog that was waiting to turn into a princess if only the right people gave it a kiss.

It was October 2017, and we called Jill, reserved a room at the Stickett Inn, and drove to the property. The leaves were a sumptuous canvas of oranges, reds, and yellows. We drove deep into the countryside, which was dense with woods. It was like diving into a brochure inviting people to escape their humdrum everyday lives into the fiery exhilaration of the fall colors. Then we found the address and turned into the little circular driveway. My first impression was better than Jill's. Our Realtor simply said, "Huh, this is the house you like?"

I think she meant it as a statement, but it came out as a question.

I said, "I like the property a lot."

I might as well have said it had a good personality.

"Next door is thirty-five acres," said Jill, who had done her homework. "The owner just hunts there. Across the street is a summer camp that at this point seems mostly unused other than the occasional caretaker."

"So we won't see anyone unless we want to," I said.

"Exactly."

The property was spectacular. Both Tim and I smiled at each other as we looked in all directions and took in the *space* that had inspired this endeavor. The woods were thick and full of life and nourishment for the soul. There was a fairly extensive lawn and wild hydrangeas everywhere. The air was chilled and clean. It was quiet. Birds squawked, telling each other there were newbies in the driveway. I remembered once reading in Thoreau's journal that he came to the woods like "a hungry man to a crust of bread." I saw that in Tim's eyes. I was more like a woman arriving at a restorative yoga class.

The house was less impressive.

"The plants look like they do in the picture," I said gamely as we stared at the exterior.

A lot of it was falling apart. The roof looked bad, and the stucco walls were chipped and peeling off in places. Jill waited silently, reminding me of a gallery owner who can't believe two people like the worst painting on display but doesn't want to interrupt a potential sale.

"It's not dilapidated," I said.

"It needs work," Tim said.

"Love and care," I added.

"It's not without charm," Tim said. "Let's look inside."

Look Past the Crap

Going inside anyplace for the first time is always a revelation. A new classroom. A boyfriend's apartment. Your kid's bedroom after they have rearranged the furniture. A house you're thinking of buying. And this place was no exception.

Jill unlocked the door and let me and Tim lead the way into an experience that fell somewhere between "Wow" and "What the actual fuck." Instead of saying "Welcome," the first impression was more of a matter-of-fact "Here I am." The great Dramatics R & B song from the early 1970s "Whatcha See Is Whatcha Get" should have been playing at that moment.

If what you're looking for is real loving
Then what you see is what you get

Why do people fall in love with a house? (I'll get to that.) Actually, the more appropriate question is why do people vacate a house with all their belongings left exactly as they were the moment they shut the door?

The whole front room where we stood—the living room, I suppose—was crammed full of furniture. It was old, musty, molded, ripped, rodent and bug infested. And on top of the furniture and on the walls was stuff. My eyes were drawn to the dark wood stairs, where I saw an outdoor flower box full of rotted silk flowers. The walls were decorated with deer heads that were themselves in various states of decay and decomposition. The kitchen was in the same condition. The ceiling dropped, making it feel small and close, and the counters, drawers, and cabinets were full of more stuff. I saw dirty dishes in the sink. All of it old, old, old. And then . . .

"Tim, come look at this," I said.

He walked in and found me standing in front of an open cabinet, holding a box of Cheerios.

"Cereal!" I said. "For God's sake. There is still cereal here."

Tim shrugged, unfazed.

"Let's look upstairs," he said.

There, in the loft, we found more of the same, and just more. Beds, clothes, rugs. Back downstairs, the built-in bed in the primary bedroom was a tangle of jungle-print bedding still on the mattress with matching curtains.

"Timmy, will you look at this!" I said from the bathroom.

He stood in the doorway. I was shaking my head in disbelief.

"Freaking shampoo and soap!" I said. "It's all still here. Whoever lived here, it's like they were just raptured up."

As we continued our exploration, I grew more and more curious about the people who had lived here and what happened to them that they left everything. People talk about staging homes. This was anti-staging. Something about the scene felt dire and sad. There was a story here, but it had been left unfinished. The last act was a blank page.

I am sure that explains why, when I looked over at Tim, I saw something I didn't expect: a smile on his face.

"I see that grin," I said. "What are you thinking?"

"I love the fireplace," he said. "And the pine paneling."

"Yes . . . and??"

"It's exactly what I was looking for."

The slight grin on my husband's face and the glint in his eyes were a window into his brain, and I saw exactly what he was thinking. It wasn't a magic trick. I knew Tim. His impressive biography states that he is a producer, director, and Emmy Award–winning actor, and goes on to list a sick number of accomplishments in film, in television, and on the stage, including the founding of two successful theaters in Sacramento, California: the Fantasy Theatre (also named the honorary state children's theater of California) and the B Street Theatre. That means building sets has been a major part of his life.

When he starts whistling "If I Had a Hammer," watch out. I have seen him sit down in front of his computer and look up the schematics for something he wants to do, and the next thing I know we're figuring out how to do it.

I was a bit more hesitant. I wasn't saying no to the house, but my enthusiasm was tamped down by all the stuff—the claustrophobic amount of furniture, the faded silk flowers, the stale cereal in the cabinet, the used and cracking bars of soap in the shower. Just all the stuff. And the gawd-awful smell. But wherever I turned, Tim's smile was shining a light on the potential. I saw it, too. I just had to walk around and find it.

While I did, I asked questions. How bad is this room? How bad are the floors? Will the walls hold up? What's going on with the roof? Can we get rid of the odor? Then there were the basics: Were we on a septic tank or something else? (I didn't know what else there could be but I had seen an outhouse and I just didn't want to go there, literally.) What was the status of the well? Would we run out of water? Were we stepping into a disaster or a dream?

Then, as I stared up at one of the rotting deer heads on the wall, a lifetime of therapy kicked in and I thought I could do something here. I just had to look past the crap and see the possibilities, not the problems.

That's a lesson for our times. A lesson for the ages.

How many times in my life had I told myself to look past the crap?

I had gone through the nose job, the Botox and the fillers, the hair color and the painted-on cleavage when I was a kid, and all the other crazy things I had done to myself over the years to get to who I am authentically inside and outside. What I do for a living requires me to dig through the layers to find the essence of a character. I have spent my entire life trying to see past the crap and get to the heart of everything.

I slipped my arm through my husband's, knowing this place

would be the next item on the list. We would tackle this project together.

"What do you think of the smell?" I asked, my expression communicating the way I felt about it.

Reaching deep into our familial lexicon, he pulled out a favorite: "Buh-sgus-teen."

Perfect. I agreed. We decided to make an offer.

An Offer and a Gentleman

We put in the offer around Thanksgiving and were done by the first week of January 2019. Tim and I were ecstatic. Not only was the house ours, but it had also passed all inspections.

Each of us helped the other stay calm while we went through the process, which was like taking the house to a doctor for a thorough checkup after thirty years of bad eating habits, chronic smoking, excessive drinking, unbridled drug use, and general neglect, and hoping and praying for a report of good health.

We had to be sure we weren't being idiots and buying a place that was going to cost hundreds of thousands of dollars to get up to speed. If that was the case, we might as well have bought a newer place. We might as well have won the lottery, too. The reality of our finances was more Hofbräu than Hollywood. We were blessed with enough money from Tim's Directors Guild retirement to pay for the place, but where the real estate sections of the *Los Angeles Times* and the *New York Times* regularly featured costars, colleagues, and acquaintances of ours selling and buying real estate in the tens of millions of dollars, we got this little house on the prairie for slightly more than ninety thousand dollars—beer money for George Clooney.

And a champagne celebration for the two of us. For the longest time, we had been telling each other that we needed to own something. Neither of us had owned a home in a while because we had been through divorces and real estate disasters exacerbated by the recession, and we thought it was important to claim ownership of a little patch of this planet that would grow in value and provide security in the event of a "God forbid."

The transaction was not covered in the *Times*, *People* magazine, or the *New York Post*'s Page Six. It barely made the MLS. Zillow simply noted the house was "off market"—the same status Tim and I had claimed since meeting seven years earlier. The fact that we were, in this first month of 2019, happily married (to each other) and buying a run-down home in the country (together) was proof that life is a constantly unfolding series of surprises and aha moments. Especially when it comes to marriage. Not that I ever claimed to have that whole thing figured out.

As role models, my parents were examples of people who had partnered for life. Just not with each other. My dad, actor and comedian Paul Gilbert, was married a legendary thirteen times. My mother, dancer and actress Barbara Crane, has exchanged I-dos several times, and her sister made at least as many trips up and down the aisle as my mom, if not more. What can I say? We are optimists. We are passionate. And we believe in love. But we should come with a warning label because we are kind of unlucky once we find it.

At least that's the way I felt until Tim came into my life. A few years before him, I was with my second husband, actor Bruce Box-leitner, raising our then-teenage son, Michael, and preparing to go on tour in the musical *Little House on the Prairie*. From 1974 to 1983, I had played Laura Ingalls Wilder in the TV series based on her beloved books. Now I was starring as her mother. Before we completed previews at the Paper Mill Playhouse in New Jersey, my back started to hurt to the point where I couldn't function. Then the pain migrated into my right leg. A neurosurgeon diagnosed me with a herniated disc in my lower back, my L5-S1. I'd already been through surgery in 2003 for a bad disc in my neck, so I knew what lay ahead: a lot of pain and discomfort. Ugh.

Ordered to bed, I missed the last few shows in New Jersey but returned to the lineup in time for the twenty-six-city national tour, starting in Minneapolis. The show was a family-oriented crowd-pleaser. Audiences laughed, cried, and cheered performances. But behind the scenes, this heartwarming musical felt like a death trap. The fake snow, or "snoap" as we called it, made the stage so slippery that, at one point or another, all the actors fell flat on their keister as they entered. One person broke a rib. Another tore their meniscus. After I went sprawling across the stage, my back pain became nearly unbearable.

Every couple of weeks, I went to a local hospital for steroids. Sometimes when I stepped onstage, my leg gave out from under me and I would need an epidural nerve block and a few days off. Several times I left the theater in an ambulance. Once the tour finally ended, I returned home and saw Dr. Robert Bray, who had operated on my neck in 2003. After a bunch of X-rays, he walked into the exam room and said, "Did you drive yourself here?"

"Yes," I said.

"Well, you're going to have to drive home very slowly and be careful what you do."

"Huh?"

"Your back is broken," he said.

He threw a slide up on the screen, where I saw a black-and-white picture of my spine. Each vertebra was clear—and so was a piece of bone that was floating in my back.

"That?" I asked, pointing to the breakaway bone.

"That." Dr. Bray nodded.

He pointed to the disc where it had come from; it was obliterated. Surgery followed, and when my husband was called to bring me home, he asked if I could instead hire a car or ask a friend. My massage therapist and dear friend Phillip (aka Lord Torgue Ward; don't ask) picked me up. Bruce's response, or lack thereof, gave me plenty to think about during the long, slow recovery.

I knew postsurgical care and compassion was not Bruce's specialty. I made up for it. I was Superwoman. I had spent our entire relationship taking care of him and everyone else, including myself, and it spoke volumes about who I was at that time, and also who he was. That dynamic worked well for us for many years, but things had changed for me. I could recover without his support and compassion, but the question I suddenly asked myself was, *Why?* Why was it okay for me not to be cared for? What made me feel that I didn't deserve to have that in my life?

My recovery involved learning to walk again, and when struggling with something so basic, so automatic, something that I had learned when I was ten months old and never thought about again until I was in my mid-forties, I was reminded not to take anything in life for granted, including my marriage.

Life is full of traffic signals and I was seeing a lot of red lights.

At the end of the year, we vacationed on Hawaii's big island for the first time. Michael went with us, and the next youngest of our four sons, Dakota, also joined us there after bouncing out of marine boot camp with a medical discharge for shin splints. That whole trip Bruce was basically on his own schedule, having lunch when we went down to the beach, resting in the room when we ate lunch on the beach, and so on. There was just this weird, uncomfortable distance. All of us were together, though, the day we went for a tour of Volcanoes National Park and ended up at night at the edge of a volcano, watching the bewitching red lava flow down the mountain and into the water, where it created new land right in front of our eyes.

The symbolism was not lost on me. When I reached for Bruce's hand, he pushed mine away. The boys saw it. They came up on either side of me and took my hands. As hard as it was to admit, I knew if I was going to march forward into new land, it was going to be with the support of my family but without Bruce. That was just reality. Neither of us was truly happy, and after spending years going in and out of therapy alone and as a couple, I didn't see the situation changing.

Our separation was traumatic for family and friends alike, not to mention Bruce and me. All of us went through a period of soul searching and suffering, but eventually things quieted down. Intent on avoiding a fight, Bruce and I decided on a mediator instead of hiring lawyers. The mediator blocked out three days. However, Bruce and I had already promised to simply walk away and not take or demand anything from each other. As a result, our mediation lasted three hours. We had lunch together at Jerry's Deli and walked away friends.

I mourned the end of the longest relationship of my life. It was a sad and painful time. But I wasn't the only one who suffered. Our teenage son Michael struggled with the breakup. Seeing him in pain was worse than anything I experienced. Therapy helped all of us. So did talking, hugging, crying, and being patient and forgiving of one another. Eventually the trauma subsided. Wounds began to heal. And we moved forward.

I moved way too fast. Feeling like I had been tamped down and muzzled for far too long, I raced into my new relationship status, trying to make up for lost time and recapture the freedom I remembered from my youth. I knew I wasn't a kid anymore, but I wasn't ready or willing to concede any ground. All women experience enormous pressure to look and stay young and attractive but, as I discovered, being a single woman in your forties in Los Angeles is a whole different league of pressure, and being an actress looking for work in an industry obsessed with youth ratchets that up even further.

I reacted as many women I encountered did: I attempted to freeze everything in place. I wrote my own version of *Middle Age Crazy*, the 1980 movie starring Bruce Dern as a real estate developer who buys a Porsche and gets a Dallas Cowboys cheerleader girlfriend after turning forty. I had Botox, fillers, recolored my hair, and bought a Mustang convertible at the urging of the slightly younger but wildly inappropriate French dude I began dating.

I told myself that he was fresh, fun, and proof that I was still desirable. But really he was all the bad behaviors of anyone with whom I had ever been involved, married or otherwise, rolled into one package. He was every lesson I refused to learn. He had a little bit of my first husband, Bo Brinkman; a little bit of hubby number two, Bruce; some of Rob Lowe's bad-boy qualities; and so on. And all the wrong things from everybody.

He was mean.

He was not generous.

He was self-centered.

He was vain.

He was judgmental.

He was chauvinistic.

He was xenophobic.

He was uber-conservative politically.

And he was obvious about it.

During a vacation in Marrakesh, we came upon a group of children begging for money. Moved by the plight of these young human beings, many of whom I saw were sick or suffering from some kind of affliction, I reached into my pocket. He stopped me.

"Don't give these children your monies," he scoffed. "They're faking."

"They're sick," I countered. "They have no fingers."

"I don't care," he said.

He didn't—and that was infuriating. To his credit (and mine, I suppose), he was a good-looking guy, and from a truly lovely family, so I held on to the threads of possibilities. But we were like oil and water: interesting for a minute but not much beyond that. At one point, my mother had a gathering at her house so that everyone in the family could meet the new guy in my life and he showed up wearing a T-shirt that had the word *Snatch* on it.

We understood it referred to the 2000 Guy Ritchie movie. But we knew the word also referred to something else, and we were aghast at the fact that he thought it was okay to wear the shirt to this Sunday brunch . . . at my MOTHER'S HOUSE!

The relationship lasted pretty much the duration of my time on *Dancing with the Stars*. That was the other thing that skewed my life the wrong way. I was in this relationship with a young, inappropriate French dude, my face was frozen in time, and I got invited to be part of the ultimate spray-tan-glitter-fake-hair-fake-everything festival of falsity, except for the fact I was training nonstop and telling myself that I had to do this *farkakte* show to prove that my back was healed and I could do anything I wanted.

It was hands-down the most agonizing, painful, physical, emotional, exhausting thing I had done in my life at that point, and I was doing it without any support from my most handsome and even more self-centered and insensitive Frenchman, who, when he did surface, sloughed off my aches and complaints with a disdaining "Pfft."

On the show, I partnered with dance pro Maksim Chmerkovskiy, a demanding, generous, warm, temperamental, funny, difficult, charming, talented, and emotional perfectionist whom I adore to this day. Our paso doble was one of the hardest things I had ever tried to learn. It proved that I really could tackle anything I put my mind to, and my body would follow, sometimes reluctantly, but damn it, it did as requested. On the live broadcast, our paso started with a surprisingly impressive combination of speed, precision, and Spanish flair. But as Maks and I approached the climactic drop spin, I got too close to him and catastrophe struck. His feet caught my head and neck, and suddenly the six-foot-two-inch Ukrainian went flying while I screamed in pain.

Though my instinct was to put on a tough face and tell everyone I was fine, I knew it was bad. An ambulance took me to the hospital, where I was diagnosed with a severe concussion and whiplash and sent home to rest. I missed the results episode the next night. I also missed the larger point. My *Dancing* injuries were only the most immediate problems I faced. My whole life was spinning out of control.

And that was so typical of me at the time.

I was making things more difficult than they needed to be.

My brain was always going a million miles an hour.

The rest of me was going the same speed.

Everything in me going and doing and moving and trying to prove something. Except my forehead. It was frozen.

Then one day my patio roof literally collapsed on me. I had walked outside with my kids to show them a handful of potted plants I had just bought. As I explained I was thinking about hanging them on the posts that supported the patio roof, there was a loud crack. Suddenly and without warning, the eight-hundred-pound roof collapsed on top of us. My first concern was the kids. I asked if they were okay.

"Fine, Mom," came the response. "Are you all right?"

I thought I was, but my son Michael shook his head.

"Mom, you're bleeding!" he said.

Indeed, there was blood trickling down my face. I went back to the ER. I got a few stitches in my head. I was also diagnosed with another concussion and once again told to rest. But while prone in a dark bedroom, I realized there was more to recovering from this mishap. The roof's collapsing on me was a none-too-subtle message from God. She was literally smacking me in the head and asking what I was doing with my life. *Wake up, Melissa!*

You're driving a Mustang convertible.

Your face doesn't move.

Your boobs are too big.

You're with the wrong guy.

The list went on and on.

The next day I was lying in bed with an ice pack on my head, the throbbing of pain serving as an imperative for the need to make changes. My life clearly wasn't working. I couldn't be with inappropriate dudes anymore. I couldn't continue to do these things to my face and my body. I had to figure out who I was and where I was headed and what was good and healthy for me.

I called the Frenchman, who was soon going to visit me from his place in Paris. I remember his picking up on my tone and beating me to the punch.

"I'm not coming anymore," he said.

"No," I said, correcting him. "I am canceling your ticket."

And that was that. I washed my hands of him and declared there would be no more dating in my life for the foreseeable future. I wasn't just saying that, either. There were a couple of fun, casual fellas hanging around, but I didn't trust myself. Rather than meet new people and populate my life with handsome distractions, I needed to find myself. I was forty-eight years old. Fifty was just down the block and around the corner. It was time.

I started hanging out with Daniel Robb, my gay best friend—my GBF. He was sane, fun, and supportive. If I thought I looked good, he said I was on fire. If I felt off, he said, "Girl, I only wish I had what you have." One night we made plans to go disco dancing at a local nightclub with a group of his friends. Daniel and I arranged to get together beforehand to play board games and have dinner at a restaurant. When we got to the restaurant, though, it was closed. I knew a cool little bar nearby that didn't get busy and loud until about ten or eleven o'clock, so we went there.

It was only eight when Daniel and I walked in, and the place was empty and quiet, as I had anticipated. As I ordered a cranberry club soda, Danny realized that he had forgotten his phone at my house. Since I lived only ten minutes away, he took off, leaving me alone in the bar. I was immediately uncomfortable. Even though I was the only person there other than the bartender, I never went to a bar alone. If I was traveling, I might go downstairs to the restaurant and sit by myself, but I would have a book and no intention of talking to anybody.

Now I was by myself, without a book, and nervous someone might walk in and want to talk to me, God forbid. And then, of course, someone did.

As I waited for Danny, a guy walked into the bar with a slice of pizza and sat about five or six stools down from me. I looked at him out of the corner of my eye. It was Tim. I recognized him. We had met at the Emmy Awards in 1991, the year he won an Emmy for his work on *thirtysomething*. I was there participating in a tribute to Michael Landon, who had passed away earlier that year. Tim would later claim that we had met before that and I was rude to him, but I couldn't remember that . . . and since I have no memory of that alleged encounter . . . it never happened.

But we had connected more recently the way people did in 2012—on Facebook. Tim had accepted my friend request about ten days earlier, which kind of meant that we did know each other. And because I am not rude, I thought I should strike up a conversation, except I'm not good at instigating small talk. I tend to say something stupid or get tongue-tied, and then my voice will squeak because I'm terribly shy. I also have terrible social anxiety and worry that no one will want to talk to me. But something about this situation was different.

I worked up my nerve and said, "Tim?"

He turned around. "Yes?"

"It's Melissa Gilbert. You just accepted my friend request on Facebook."

He nodded, and we started to talk. Gradually, I leaned in until I moved one stool closer to him. He did the same. We played that game until we were sitting next to each other and engrossed in conversation. The bar could have been filled with people and a rock band playing live and we wouldn't have noticed. In fact, when I looked around, Danny was there, with all of his friends who were supposed to meet us at the disco. They were waiting for me. Apparently hours had passed. I gave him a look that said, "I don't know what's going on. Help me! What am I doing?"

Taking care not to interrupt, Danny finally sidled over to me and widened his eyes, as if to ask what was going on.

"I don't want to do this," I whispered. "I've lost my mind. But he's cute, right?"

Later, Danny said that he could see cartoonlike stars coming out of Tim's eyes. I was sure they had matched mine. It was clear the two of us were cooked. Finally, Tim said he had to get going. We exchanged numbers and, on his way out of the bar, Tim gave my right earlobe a gentle tug, which turned me into a puddle of mush right there on my bar stool. My friends and I went to the club and danced until two a.m. I was thinking about Tim when I woke up later that morning around ten and immediately reached for my phone.

Do you want to meet for brunch? I texted.

I was just texting you the same thing, he replied.

From then on, I didn't have a single moment where I thought I wasn't sure or that connecting with Tim wasn't great. When we started dating, he was directing the pilot for the ABC Family drama *The Fosters* and worked all night, so we met for breakfast after he finished on the set. One morning he walked into the restaurant holding a huge bouquet of flowers and all the women there sighed out loud dreamily. Each time I visited him on the set, both the cast and crew told me how much they loved him.

I didn't need to be convinced. Tim was smart and deeply talented. I found myself learning from him, which was exciting. He also made me laugh so hard my legs would buckle. Within two months of meeting in that bar, both of us knew we were serious about each other. But we didn't talk about it. I invited him to my mother's house for Thanksgiving, and he fit right in. It was like we were two souls who had just been waiting to find each other.

Many years before, when I was going through a really rough patch in my first-ever relationship, my friend Bunny Ladge Gottfried had remarked, "You know, Melissa, there are easier relationships out there." Although I believed that was true, I didn't think I would ever find that person until I met Tim. But then, as is always the case when something seems too good to be true, came the speed bump.

Ask Me Again in the Morning

Maybe we should hang on to this," Tim said, referring to the perfectly sized yet truly fugly puke-green floral sectional sofa in the living room.

To me, it was an unmitigated assault on the senses. It smelled, I could almost hear the mites running around in it, and it hurt my eyes to look at. I was shaking my head before I even spoke.

"Are you nuts?" I asked. "It's wet. It's mildewed. It's gross. It's probably full of people's sloughed-off skin cells and God knows what else . . . It has got to go."

To which Tim responded, "Aside from all that?"

It was January 2019, and the house was ours. So was the mess in and around it. And so was the work that needed to be done to make the place livable. All the inspections we had done prior to the purchase and afterward for our peace of mind had come back better and better, in context, of course. One of the inspectors, picking up on my anxiety, had said, "Don't worry. It's really not as bad as it looks." Indeed, despite some minor leaks, the roof inspector had given us a thumbs-up. The guy who had checked the well had given our water an A+. The level, pressure, and taste were perfect.

"It's pure and clean," he said.

When I finally tasted it, I was downright giddy. It was cold and refreshing, with just the right taste—not too soft and not too hard. People in LA paid small fortunes to put in systems that made their water taste the way nature had provided it to us for free. I was equally and inexplicably delighted when the plumber informed us that we had a cesspool and not a septic tank, and it worked fine. It was located under the outhouse.

"The outhouse?" I said.

He nodded toward the structure.

"Yep, and you can use that, too."

"Not if I don't have to," I said, wincing. Yes, the Ingalls family had an outhouse on the prairie, but that was a TV show! This was real life, and there was no way I was going in that nasty, dark, rickety, smelly structure . . . EVER!

It was pretty clear that Tim and I would not be able to start living there anytime soon, and as I shivered in the near-freezing temperatures, the plumber explained that whenever we left for any length of time, we had to drain the whole house and put antifreeze in the toilets and sinks. Drain the house?! I thought as I nodded like I knew what he meant and how to do that; Tim did the same thing later when I relayed that information to him.

"Right, just pour antifreeze into the toilet bowl, maybe?" he said, turning the statement into a question.

I shook my head, then read the notes I'd feverishly typed into my iPhone.

"No, we have to turn off power to the water pump; completely drain the water heater, then turn it off; turn off the water to the toilets, the sinks, and the bathtub; then pour RV antifreeze in all of them. It will fill the pipes, protect everything from freezing and cracking, and we'll be good."

"Okay, Halfpint," he said.

The house had no heat. When I say "no heat," I mean no heating system. It was seasonal only, not year-round. So, before we could start clearing it out, Tim bought enormous propane heaters to warm us. These heaters worked but were extremely loud, so there was an awful lot of yelling those first few days, but it was better than freezing our tushies off. We also slipped on face masks, gloves, and protective clothing (foreshadowing much?). The interior was a malodorous mix of mildew, rodent excrement, and general fetidness that we didn't want going directly into our lungs. We tossed nearly everything the people had left in an enormous dumpster. Chairs, tables, rotting deer heads, pictures on the walls, dishes, glasses, food, clothes, newspapers, broken toys . . . all of it went. The job took four days. After we started, Tim was called to work and left the last three days of the exorcism to me and our assistant at the time. Two women in the woods, wielding axes, flexing our muscles, and frequently shrieking our disgust to each other.

In order to get the built-in king-size bed in the master out of the house, we tackled it with hatchets. When we opened it up, dozens of mice scurried out, their cozy home suddenly attacked. I caught as many as possible with the nearest implement, which turned out to be an old Crock-Pot, and carried them outside, apologizing for upsetting their situation and wishing them well. Shelves of crap followed, along with a dollhouse and several bottles of holy water . . . yes, holy water.

"Are you kidding me?" I exclaimed after finding those. "Why? Please explain to me, why holy water. What happened here?!"

I couldn't stop thinking about the people who had lived in this house. Who were they? Why had they gone? Where had they gone? We worked nonstop, arriving early in the morning and driving back down to the city at night.

Tim and I noticed a small plaque embedded in the stone fireplace. It had some sort of initials and a date carved in it, "FI-GOW-IE-1958," very intentional, not random. I looked it up and asked the town's local historian if she knew what it meant. She didn't know; in fact, nobody knew. Someone remembered an elderly woman once living in the place, and she was said to be a lovely Italian or German woman. That just gilded the mystery. I'd been told rumors about Nazis and Nazi sympathizers settling in the area in the forties, which was interesting, since this neck of the woods became a mainstay for New York City Jews on summer vacation.

We were a stone's throw from Grossinger's, the most popular of the Catskill resorts. I went there a few times as a kid. Both my father, Paul Gilbert, and my grandfather Harry Crane had entertained there. This was before my grandfather co-created Jackie Gleason's classic TV series *The Honeymooners* and became a top comedy writer. The last time I had gone there was to see my friend Anthony Newley perform in the eighties. Classic memories—and now I was back in the hood.

I sensed that you could travel thousands of miles in life, as I had, and never go more than a few blocks.

Because someone once told me that you're supposed to keep one or two things that belonged to the house, we rehabbed a couple of kitchen chairs, some wineglasses, and a funky porcelain figurine of a rooster. In a crawl space that appeared when we demoed the dropped kitchen ceiling, we also found a bottle of Seagram's and a nudie magazine from the seventies. Those stayed, too.

Finally, the place was empty. Tim and I were exhausted, in a good way. We had done a ton of work and we still had a ton of work ahead of us before the place would be even close to inhabitable. But it felt good. It had good vibes. The bones were strong and sturdy. It was ready to be turned into a home.

I'd had that same feeling once before, early in my relationship with Tim. Following that first Thanksgiving at my mom's, we were figuring out plans for Christmas. We wanted to spend the holiday together. I already had a gut feeling that I could have a real partnership with this guy. Like the house, the bones of the relationship were strong and sturdy, and I had no intention of being without Tim for the rest of this lifetime and beyond.

Tim felt the same way about me. But he feared there might be a problem. He was only in LA temporarily. He had moved to Michigan after a truly nasty divorce set him back both emotionally and financially. He'd bought a house at the peak of the bubble and had to sell during the recession. His finances were as ugly as mine following my split from Bruce. To recover, Tim had moved back to his home state (he had graduated from East Lansing High School in 1975) and reshaped his life to be small, manageable, and personal. Which I admired—and envied more than a little bit.

"The good news is that I am really into you," he said. "But the bad news is that I live in Michigan."

"That's not bad news," I said, and then, a moment later, added, in my best Tina Fey imitation, "I want to go to there. Please get me out of LA!!"

"Really?" he asked.

"Seriously. I can't move my forehead—and that's not okay. I have a feeling that I'm going to want to move it more in the future. I'd like to go someplace where that's possible."

Tim lived in a small, one-bedroom cabin-like home on a lake in Holly, Michigan. Michael and I went there for Christmas, and then the three of us spent about a week over New Year's at his childhood friend Pete Benington's cabin about three hours north. The place and surrounding winterscape were gorgeous, and the Beningtons welcomed us with open arms. Literally. They didn't do frou-frou Hollywood air-kisses in this part of the country. Their hugs were warm and genuine.

There were nine kids in the Benington family, including Casey, Tim's BFF. Tim became the tenth when his family sort of exploded and everyone went their separate ways. Mrs. Benington—Barb, or GB—a widower raising nine children, took Tim in as a high schooler. She was a head surgical nurse, a devoted Catholic, and an AIDS activist who, from the very beginning of the crisis, cared for people afflicted with that horrid disease. She stepped in to help when most people would not. When most people were terrified that somehow they might catch it. Or worse, didn't care about some "gay cancer." Barb was a warrior for what was right, true, and best. She was that kind of lady—and, as Michael and I found out over the course of that week, they were that kind of family. We had the best time there.

Tim and I were in the guest bedroom, on New Year's Eve, and as we pulled back the comforter on the bed, Tim looked at me and said, very simply, "Marry me."

I looked across the bed and, without hesitation, said, "Okay."

We held each other at the foot of the bed for a long time and then I looked up at him and said, "Will you please do me a favor? Will you please ask me again in the morning when we are fully awake, fresh, and clearheaded?" He laughed and said, "Of course."

We got in bed.

Lights were turned off.

We kissed, said *I love you*, and then turned over and went to sleep in spoons just like we had every night before and have every night since.

I would love to tell you that I stayed up all night worrying about whether I was making the right decision. Or that I was creating a very sensible list of pros and cons in my head and that I was weighing those pros and cons logically and methodically. The truth is, I slept like a baby that night. I slept like that because I knew in my skin, in my bones, and in my soul that we were meant to be together. Yes, ours was a union of passion and fire and all those fun exciting things, but at its core there was/is the inevitability of two souls that have met and re-met over several lifetimes. It's kind of hard to put into words. I'll just say that it felt . . . well . . . like destiny.

Some eight hours later, I opened my eyes and there was Tim, looking right at me, his beautiful blue-green eyes twinkling.

"Will you marry me?" he asked.

I smiled. "Yes, of course I will."

Meshuggeneh for Michigan

Before we told anyone, Tim spoke with Michael.

"How would you feel if I asked your mom to marry me?" he asked.

My son gave him an enormously enthusiastic hug and it deepened the already incredible relationship between the two of them.

When we got back to LA, a dinner was planned for all of our seven kids to meet and hopefully give their blessings to our forthcoming union. Tim had three children from his previous marriages, Willy, Daisy, and Sam, and I had my posse of four boys from my previous marriages, Dakota, Michael, Sam, and Lee. As we got ready for dinner, I told Tim that I had blended a family before and assured him, "I know how to do this. And since our offspring are all grown-up, I think this time will be even easier."

I was wrong. At our first family dinner, which was attended by all except Sam Busfield, who was out of town, I realized that blending *this* family was going to be more of a challenge than I had anticipated. Tim's kids were adults with their own fully formed ideas about relationships, family, and life. They were also still nursing some very hurt feelings about stuff in the past, and I realized that I had to tread very lightly.

My boys were more accepting. They had been to this rodeo before and being party to the Gilbert side of the family had taught them that even when shit happens, as it inevitably does to everyone, it may not turn out to be as horrible as you first think. It may even contain some valuable lessons that lighten the load you carry. Blended families are full of sensitivities and trapdoors, mine included, and as dinner that night taught me, I had to adjust my expectations and allow everyone to be who they need to be and feel whatever they need to feel.

Our blended family would have moments of togetherness and fun in the future, but for now, our effort at meeting and greeting and *blending* was an important lesson for me in learning to love fully without an attachment to the result.

Tim and I decided on a simple, small wedding. I had trouble finding a dress that I liked. I looked for months. I tried white, but for my third wedding it seemed ironic. I tried baby pink and powder blue, but they seemed immature. Black was too foreboding for such a happy, auspicious occasion. One day my mom suggested Morgane Le Fay, one of her favorite designers, and off we went to the Morgane Le Fay store in Santa Monica.

We walked in the door and both of our mouths dropped open. There it was, the first dress we saw: a gorgeous, strapless, layered chiffon gown in the most beautiful shade of deep red either of us had ever seen. Both of us had the same thought. *Red!* It was the perfect color for a third wedding ceremony. It was the color of love and passion . . . and just a little bit saucy.

With that settled, we got on with the main event. At the end of April 2013, Tim and I drove up the California coast to the San Ysidro Ranch in Montecito, where, after a tremendous rainstorm, we were blessed with a beautiful blue sky and breathtaking ocean view. We traded loving vows, exchanged rings, shared our favorite poems in front of a forever vista that captured everything we felt.

Tim was so incredibly handsome in his blue suit, and I felt like a queen in my dress. There were no guests, virtually no expense, and absolutely no drama. It was just the two of us, and then we were Mr. and Mrs. Busfield.

Next up was moving to Michigan. I was so excited for this new adventure. On our way to the lake house in Holly the previous December, Tim and I had driven through a bunch of adorable little towns. Each town looked more like Bedford Falls than the one before. I loved it when we stopped and walked the Main Streets. With the big chain stores outside of town, these smaller, family-owned stores had personality and were filled with unique treasures. No two places were alike. People said hello, and when they offered to help us find something, they weren't talking only about the merchandise in their establishments. We got suggestions on where to eat and shop, directions to the next town, and tips on places to stop for pasties, the delicious Michigan version of hand pies.

Even though it was winter then, the countryside was gorgeous. Farms stretched out along the highway. Barns were really red and girded by silver grain silos. Cows munched a leisurely lunch or afternoon snack, oblivious to the cold. I felt like I had driven from Hollywood straight into a Hallmark greeting card.

Michigan's state motto—*Si Quaeris Peninsulam Amoenam, Circumspice*—when translated to English from Latin, means "If you are seeking a pleasant peninsula, look around you." I was doing that from the car window, and I saw it there for me.

As spring tiptoed into the north, Tim and I looked in various towns for a place to live and eventually stumbled upon a beautiful Victorian home in Howell, a town of less than ten thousand people between East Lansing, Detroit, Ann Arbor, and Flint. The house, which dated back to the 1800s, had been lovingly restored and amazingly was for rent. We weren't sure how long we wanted to stay, so we thought it best not to buy.

After signing a lease, we returned to LA, packed everything, and hired movers. Just as we set our GPS, we encountered a hiccup. Tim was hired as the executive producer in charge of production on *Mind Games*, a new ABC drama with Christian Slater and Steve Zahn. It was a plum job, but the show shot in Chicago, and Tim was going to have to spend anywhere from nine to thirteen weeks there, and perhaps more if they got picked up for more episodes, which they did.

So Tim jetted off to Chicago in search of a temporary place while I ran point with the movers. Once the truck was loaded, Michael and I and our two dogs, two cats, and sugar glider drove to Michigan via Austin, Texas, where we visited with Dakota and his then-girlfriend, now-wife, Marissa, and rendezvoused with Tim, whose father also lived there at the time. From there, we stopped in St. Louis, dropped Tim at the town house he'd rented in Chicago, and met up with the moving truck in Howell.

A perfectly straight line, if you ask me.

The movers unpacked and put away a lot of our belongings, but I was still living with boxes for weeks. That was not altogether bad or inconvenient. I have had therapists who recommend putting my life in boxes, unpacking what I need, and discarding the excess. At least the bedrooms, bathrooms, and kitchen were mostly done and eminently functional. From the start, this new life in Howell was as charmed as the town was charming. The doorbell of our cute Victorian rang throughout the day with people welcoming us to the neighborhood.

Here's a casserole.

We baked you cookies.

Do you like pie?

I just want to introduce myself.

If you need anything . . .

It was so opposite of LA, where the joke is that you only meet your neighbors after an earthquake—and then it's four in the morning and everyone is in their underwear.

I was able to walk the few blocks into town. A couple of restaurants became new favorites and I enjoyed poking my head into shops. Life was simple, personal, intimate, and very different from LA. I melted right into the slow lane.

Michael did not have a similarly smooth adjustment. Before the move, he was headed for his senior year in high school. It was a crappy time to change schools and the difficulty was amplified by being in an entirely new part of the country. I was sympathetic. I wished we had been able to offer him the option of staying in LA until he finished high school, but we couldn't afford a home in both LA and Michigan.

I still suffered PTSD from years before when my then-middle-school-aged son, Dakota, had asked to live full-time with his dad in Texas, and though the situations were different, I wanted to do my best to get it right for Michael. I worked with my therapist, and Tim and I gave Michael options. He could stay in LA with his dad. He could live with his brothers. He could stay with my mother or my sister or even with his best friend, Bobby. He also had the choice to be homeschooled, give the Michigan school system a chance, or get his GED and start his career as an actor.

Michael chose to stick with us and pursue a career. I gave him a Mama Bear hug and then turned to Tim for reassurance that this was going to be okay.

Tim was the one who had suggested Michael get out of high school, enroll in nearby Lansing Community College, and join their theater department. He believed in learning the craft, every aspect, from building sets to standing onstage. If Michael liked it and did well, he could move to the next rung on the ladder.

"That's how I started," Tim had said. "My first role was in a children's theater. Then I studied at East Tennessee State University. Then I joined the Actors Theatre in Louisville. Then I moved to New York and was in the Circle Rep, then on Broadway. Eventually, in 1983, I moved to LA. That was forty years ago . . ."

Don't just look for a job, Tim advised. Build a career.

Michael still had a rough time. He moved into the basement and rarely came upstairs. He missed his friends and his routines.

He was depressed and lonely. For several months, he played video games and ate potato chips. I fretted and looked to my therapist back in LA for a long-distance lifeline. I had thought I understood adolescence. I knew nothing. I referred to Michael as "that Thing in the Basement." Somehow Tim kept the faith. He would talk with Michael and then assure me that the kid had a good head on his shoulders and was going to be okay.

He was right. By the end of summer, Michael was enrolled in Lansing Community College's theater program and loving it. Through one of Tim's old high school friends, he moved into his own apartment near campus (and away from us). He became good friends with a group of people from his class. He was challenged, busy, and happy.

Relieved, I refocused my energy on nesting and making the four-and-a-half-hour drive to Chicago to see Tim. More good news followed. We found out that my Sam and his wife, Andrea, were expecting . . . and it was a girl. Lulabelle Rose Boxleitner, the first grandbaby in this crazy giant blended family of ours, was due to arrive that fall. We were overjoyed.

Something else remarkable happened in the midst of all this activity: I had turned fifty. The Google alerts filled up my email months before my actual birthday. *CELEBRITIES TURNING 50 THIS YEAR. LOOK WHO'S TURNING 50! HALF-PINT REACHES HALF A CENTURY.* If I had wanted to ignore it, I couldn't have. But I didn't want to. I slipped fifty on as if it were a new outfit and stood in front of the mirror, getting used to the way it fit, which was surprisingly okay.

In the past, I had celebrated all my big birthdays—sixteen,

eighteen, twenty-one, thirty, forty—with huge blowouts. For fifty, I decided that I'd had enough crazy to last a lifetime. I thought something quiet and reflective was most appropriate for this milestone. Tim agreed, and he took me to the Meher Spiritual Center in Myrtle Beach, South Carolina. I never would have thought of it on my own. We got there and I stared at my husband with deep admiration. How did he know? *Because, ladies and gentlemen, that's Timothy Busfield.*

The Meher Spiritual Center is situated on five hundred acres of woodland, lakes, and oceanfront. We stayed in a tiny cabin that cost thirty-five dollars a night and literally unplugged and disconnected from the outside world. There were no phones, TVs, newspapers, or even classes to take. Just a quiet that was blanketed with Baba's message of love.

Our days were about rest and thought on a deeply spiritual level. Several places were preserved exactly as they had been the last time Meher Baba himself had been there in the sixties, and on Sunday, we went into what used to be his bedroom and rested our heads on his bed, a special ritual when, for a few minutes, visitors are able to share an intimate moment with Baba's spirit.

In addition to all my natural skepticism, I wasn't interested in acquiring any more or any new religion in my life, but I had been enjoying my time in this outdoor temple and relishing the rejuvenating effects of being immersed in nature for days, and so I gamely followed Tim into this bedroom. Then, when it was my turn to go in, I laid my forehead on the bed and my whole face started leaking tears, like I was binge-crying uncontrollable tears full of joy. It was the strangest, weirdest thing, and I loved it. I sailed out of there on a carpet of bliss.

If this was fifty, I thought, bring it.

Then winter hit. It was the winter of the polar vortex. I had never seen a winter like this before. It was seventeen below in our backyard. We had forty-eight inches of accumulated snow. We had to dig to get from the house to the garage. It was over my head in places. My friend Debbie Fazica had the brilliant idea of giving me a slow cooker, so that winter all I did was make stuff like loaded baked potato soup in the slow cooker, leave it warming in the kitchen, and take a mugful whenever I walked by. I must have gained thirty pounds that winter. I didn't know if I was trapped or deliriously happy.

There was nothing else to do but eat. Our friend Jeff Daniels, another Michigander, said to me, "Listen, if you get bored, go to Ann Arbor. They think they're Paris."

I laughed.

"No, really," he said. "They have a Whole Foods and a Pilates studio."

The Whole Foods intrigued me.

Pilates not so much.

What did capture my attention was the state's 2014 gubernatorial campaign. Democrat Mark Schauer was running against Republican incumbent Rick Snyder. Schauer's running mate for lieutenant governor was a former state rep and Oakland County clerk, Lisa Brown. I liked both Schauer and Brown. As a new resident, I wanted to learn more about them and the issues. Learning as much as possible was part of my DNA, as was my distrust of people who thought they already knew it all.

Slow Cooker Loaded Baked Potato Soup

6 large baking potatoes, peeled and cut into ½-inch cubes
1 large onion, chopped
3 cloves garlic, minced
1 quart chicken broth
¼ cup butter
2½ teaspoons salt
1 teaspoon pepper
1 cup heavy cream or half-and-half

1 cup shredded cheddar cheese, plus more for sprinkling
3 tablespoons chopped fresh chives, plus more for sprinkling
Sour cream
8 slices bacon, fried and crumbled

Combine the first seven ingredients in a large slow cooker and cook on high for 4 hours or low for 8 hours (the potato chunks should be tender).

Mash the mixture until the potato chunks are small enough to blend with an immersion blender. Blend until mostly smooth. You can leave it a bit chunky if you prefer, or even skip the immersion blender altogether and just mash the potatoes until the soup is slightly thickened.

Stir in the heavy cream, cheese, and chives.

Ladle into bowls and top each with a dollop of the sour cream and sprinkle with bacon crumbles, shredded cheddar, and chopped chives.

I like people who ask questions. I ask questions. I want to know what's true and what isn't. I want to know what people think. And I always want to know why. I also have this wonderful habit, as does Tim, of asking, "Why not?"

I am curious about everything. I wanted to know my neighbors, the demographics of the state, the issues that were important to people there, and the history of local and state politics. I like doing my research, and the more I read, the more I felt that this guy Rick Snyder was a typical neocon, antifeminist, anti-choice, anti-immigrant, xenophobic, homophobic, creepy climate denier.

"But how do you really feel?" Tim asked me.

We were at the gym, chugging along on neighboring treadmills. I was trying to work off the thirty pounds I'd gained in the potato soup slow cooker vortex, though by then part of my extra padding could be attributed to the discovery of another Midwestern treat—the Tater Tot hotdish. To make this tasty gem, you line a casserole dish with tater tots and then add sauteed ground beef, onion, garlic, red and green bell peppers, shredded cheese, cream of mushroom soup, and salt and pepper. Depending on the recipe, some people add corn, beans, whatever. I thought it was a pretty fantastic variation of shepherd's pie. But anyway.

"I really do think this guy Snyder is a pretty bad dude," I said. "Definitely a black hat. Not a white hat."

I mentioned something Tim already knew: Michigan had been a progressive state. In 2002, the state had elected Jennifer Granholm their first female governor. She served two terms. Hers was the office Schauer and Snyder were battling to win. The state was turning purple. It infuriated me to picture Snyder as governor for another term. To me, it spelled disaster.

I needed to support Mark and Lisa's more progressive stances.

"What should I do?" I asked Tim.

"Let's make some phone calls," he said. "We'll find them."

He found their campaign headquarters and explained his wife, Melissa Gilbert, wanted to get involved in their campaign. Surprised but delighted to hear from him, they put me to work right away. Their ground game had already started, and so I jumped in with both feet. I knocked on doors, handed out pamphlets, and made appearances with Mark and Lisa. When they were stretched, I stepped in as a surrogate speaker.

On election day, Tim was in Chicago and I was in Michigan. I got up early and voted. I spent the day with Mark and Lisa on the campaign bus. We finished at one of the large hotels in Detroit, where we decamped to a floor with all the state's Democratic candidates and regrouped in our own big suite later that evening, watching the returns. Mark and Lisa's results got bad fast, and then it was just crushing to sit there and lose.

I needed a few days of quiet and isolation to recover from the defeat and set aside all the work I was ready to do and the plans I was eager to launch. But the campaign experience left me feeling good about the way I had spent my time. I liked being with people, hearing their stories, and letting them know I would try to figure out a way to help. I was also grateful for the new friends I had made during the process, including then–Michigan state senator

Gretchen Whitmer and Steph White, a former US Army commander who headed up Equality Michigan Action Network and worked on Mark's campaign.

A few weeks later, Tim and I were the grand marshals of the Christmas parade in downtown Howell. We took along our dear pal Larry Prout Jr., a fourteen-year-old Michigan resident who came to the house one day, asking me to autograph his copy of my children's book, *Daisy and Josephine*. I ended up wanting to know this inspirational kid, who had survived more than one hundred operations after being born with spina bifida and numerous other severe problems. I had never seen a smile as big or a heart that shined as bright.

As we got ready for the parade to start, my phone suddenly started blowing up with texts. Sam's wife, Andrea, was in labor! I was beside myself with excitement and spent the parade waving with an enthusiasm that made it look like I was having the best day of my life. It was special, but I was also checking my phone constantly and trying to remain composed. I texted back and forth with Sam's mom, Kitty, as both of us waited for word. Finally, Lulabelle Rose was born, happy, healthy, and the best holiday gift ever. I squeezed my husband's arm. "How does 'Papa Tim' sound?"

He smiled. "As good as 'Granny Mel.'"

A few months later, Tim and I were planning a move to a slightly larger house in nearby Brighton, a leafy town about an hour outside of Detroit. It was early 2015, and I thought I would spend the next few months getting us situated, when those plans were interrupted by a call from Mark Schauer. After a bit of friendly catch-up, he revealed the reason for his call, asking if I would be interested in running for Congress in my district. *Congress . . . huh.* It took a moment to make sense of those words. I asked the obvious question: Why me? Mark said he had observed the way I listened to people tell me their problems and genuinely tried to help them. He felt I belonged in service.

Service was one thing, and politics was another. I was flattered. I told Mark that I needed time to think about it. I also had to speak with Tim and the other thirty-seven people I had on speed dial.

All Politics Is Personal

The chickens, the gardening, the shooing of bears, and the rest of country life that awaited me would not have been possible if things had turned out differently. I have a feeling my marriage might not have survived, either. With that being the case, I have no regrets about the eventual outcome of my campaign for Congress in Michigan's Eighth District.

Does that mean I didn't think about what it would have been like to add *congresswoman* to my résumé? And then perhaps *senator*? And then . . .

Hey, it's my fantasy.

The important thing to note is I didn't lose. I slipped into the role of candidate with an ease, focus, and sense of determination that did not surprise anyone who already knew me. Beforehand, I spoke with Tim extensively about the pros and cons of entering the race. I also talked to my kids, my mom, my sister, my publicist and agent, my business manager, friends, and, of course, a smattering of the professional politicians and organizers I had met while campaigning for Mark. Finally, I turned to Tim and said, "I'd like to give it a try. What do you think?" He pledged his support.

Having "waged a scrappy public battle," per the *Washington Post*, to become the third female president of the Screen Actors Guild, where I served from 2001 to 2005, I thought I knew what I was getting into. Not quite. Tim and I were in the midst of moving to Brighton and still unpacking boxes as new staffers, consultants, and folks from Washington's DCCC—the Democratic Congressional Campaign Committee, or D-Trip, which recruits and supports those running every two years—descended upon our little house in the big woods.

Knowing the campaign was going to consume much of my time, I imagined running things from the house to maximize the precious free time I did have with Tim. Michael was at college and Tim and I were, in many ways, still newlyweds. Alas, two's company, three's a crowd, and an entire campaign staff is chaos. We were so remote that we had satellite Internet, which was way too slow to get anything done. Cell phones and laptops ate up all the bandwidth before a single email was sent. It would have been more efficient to campaign via smoke signal.

An office was opened in nearby Howell, our old hood; a press release was readied; and in mid-August, I officially declared my candidacy. "I'm running for Congress to make life a little easier for all the families who feel they have fallen through the cracks in today's economy," I said in a statement. My Republican opponent, incumbent Mike Bishop, whose policies were at the opposite end of the spectrum from my beliefs, immediately went on the attack. His spokesperson put out a statement calling me an IRS tax cheat wanting a government paycheck and declared that my "values are out of whack with the district."

The hit left me unfazed. I did owe a significant sum of money in federal and California state taxes, as the *Detroit News* had reported nearly two months earlier, but I also had a deal with the IRS. As they instruct you to do when a tax problem arises, I called them up and said I had gone through a divorce and lost a house, and asked to work out a payment plan, which they agreed to. Even the *Detroit News*, in a follow-up story, defended me. While the writer disagreed with my so-called Obama-Pelosi politics, he said I wasn't a tax cheat. He even described his own tax issues similar to mine.

Such attacks have to be expected if you get into politics. What's the old saying? If you can't stand the heat, don't get under the blow dryer.

If anything, it made me want to fight harder to win the election. It also energized those who wanted to help me. Donations came in from George Clooney; Brad Pitt; Ben Affleck; Matthew Perry; Tom Bergeron; Rosie O'Donnell; Jennifer Garner; my sister, Sara; and a slew of other Hollywood pals and acquaintances. But it was the non-famous locals reaching out in greater numbers with smaller amounts who funded my campaign. Fundraising was the heinous reality of running for office. The whole apparatus of party support from the local to the national level is driven by how much money you raise, and I absolutely hated it.

It may be a flaw of mine, but I hate asking anyone for anything. Yet I spent up to eight hours a day dialing for dollars. Or as it's referred to officially, doing "call time."

I think it says a lot about me that I also hated being told to rein in my sense of humor, be more serious, and dress a certain way. Like the time I showed up to go give a speech at a beer garden wearing jeans, a T-shirt, and a blazer and was told to change into slacks or a dress because people from the D-Trip were going to be there. I said, "We're going to a beer garden." I also didn't like the way some people on my team were rudely dismissive of Tim's suggestions. They'd shoot down his ideas and leave it to me to tell him.

Tim hated politics, which is ironic for a guy who was on *The West Wing*. Not surprisingly, we had some of the tensest moments of our marriage during the campaign. At the same time, we shared some experiences that only underscored why we loved each other. Meeting new people with him was a pleasure. If they hated me, they were charmed by him.

For me, the best part of politics was the same thing that made it practically untenable: It was personal.

The more personal, the more I wanted to help. People were surprised when I related to their money problems. They started out thinking, *Oh, she's a celebrity, she was on TV, she's rich and famous and everything is easy for her.* But then we'd talk and I would see them relax, and then the talk would get even more real. The same was true when I met veterans. I knew they saw me as some kind of left-wing, anti-military, socialist peacenik who was far removed from the way they suffered after returning home from service. Then I told them about my father and the care—or the lack of it—he had received at the VA, how he had suffered a stroke and lived in excruciating pain for over a year, threatening to commit suicide because of it, while his VA doctors and nurses ignored his complaints, until finally he took matters into his own hands.

Afterward, those same vets and their families approached me with a new respect, that of people who suddenly shared a bond. They'd had no idea, they said. I shrugged and said that neither did I until I was forty-five years old.

Why I didn't know that fact of my life for so long was a source of friction within my family that I was only coming to terms with before I met Tim. As far as I knew, my father had a stroke when I was ten years old. A year later, my mother woke me up one morning and told me that he'd had a second stroke and had died in his sleep.

Then one night prior to publication of my 2009 memoir, *Prairie Tale*, my sister, Sara, called me. I was watching the TV show *24* with Bruce and Michael. I paused the picture and Kiefer Sutherland's face filled the screen. Why I remember that detail is beyond me. I suppose my brain froze at that exact instant and that picture was burned into my memory forever because of what came next. Sara said she was worried the book was going to cause a rift in the family. Really? I was confused as to what concerned her. She said it had to do with a mysterious secret about my father.

"But I didn't put a secret in the book," I said.

"That's the point," she said. "It's not in the book."

I hit the brakes. Full stop.

"What are you talking about?"

It turned out that her father, who had died of cancer about five years earlier, had, on his deathbed, told her that my father had shot himself in the head and that he, my mother, and my grandmother had made a pact never to tell anyone. Sara was sobbing as she revealed these facts to me. I was stunned. I couldn't believe my poor sister had carried this secret around for five years. I was just destroyed. It was like hearing that he had died all over again.

It happened in 1976, and my brother and I were told my father had a second stroke and died in his sleep. He didn't die; he *passed away*. Apparently, it was decided the details were never to be shared with us, and they weren't. It was never mentioned again. We did not attend my father's funeral or the gathering afterward. We didn't get to go through his belongings. In short, we simply did not grieve his death properly or fully. It was as if it had not happened. It was a major factor in an extraordinarily isolating and heart-breaking time in my life and played a role in a lot of my own personal issues later in life.

So when I found out the truth about his suicide years later, I lost it. Inconsolable and hysterical, I hung up with Sara and called my mother. I left her a message, asking her to call me without explaining why.

I sat up that night writing a list of questions, because I knew once my mother and I spoke the conversation would escalate and I was likely to be crazed and hysterical, and I didn't want to forget things I wanted to ask and in fact needed to know.

She called the next morning and I got straight to the point.

"I spoke to Sara last night and she said that Harold confessed to her on his deathbed that my father committed suicide, that he shot himself."

"Yes," she said in a very tiny voice. "That's true."

I erupted.

"I don't understand how you never told me this."

"You were eleven," she said.

"Yeah, but then I was eighteen. And then I was twenty-one. And then I was thirty."

I got angrier and bombarded her with rage and fury and screaming and crying to the point where there was absolutely no way for her to respond.

"I'm sorry, I can't talk to you when you're like this," she said. "You have to calm down."

I took a moment.

"Well, I just, just . . . I just don't understand how you didn't tell me."

I kept at her about that point, screaming and yelling hysterically.

Finally, she said, "I just forgot."

"You forgot?!" I screamed even louder, then, completely unhinged, said, "You *forgot* to tell me that my father shot himself in the head?!"

My family was nothing if not emotional, dramatic, loud, and brilliant, which I say with the notation that all of us applied that brilliance in different ways depending on the situation. This particular situation, as far as I was concerned, burst into flames quickly and raged for a long time. It was not easily doused by me. As someone who was adopted at birth and raised amid a loving, sometimes confusing craziness, I spent so much of my life navigating my way through the fairy dust, trying to find out the truth of who I really was, that when I did uncover something new, as had just happened, it was like the rug was pulled out from under me. I lost my balance. And I couldn't get the answers I wanted. My grandmother had dementia; my stepfather, who had been there, was dead; and my mother wouldn't communicate with me unless I calmed down—and I was the exact opposite of calm after this bombshell.

My friends Mariette Hartley and Claudette Sutherland came over and sat with me. Both of them were survivors of suicide. They were extremely generous and compassionate with me, especially Claudette, who had lost both her father and her son, in separate incidents, to suicide years earlier. When her son, Leo, had died, I didn't know what to do to help her. So I simply showed up at her house with a cashmere blanket and sat with her for days. She came to my house and returned the favor. We shared with each other the power of presence and empathy. I knew she understood everything I was feeling and going through. I could also look at her and see that there was healing ahead of me.

Thank God for everyone who supported me during that horrible time. I was and have remained immeasurably grateful. We humans can't possibly get by without helping each other. For me, though, the support of friends and therapy wasn't enough. I ended up on medication for about a year after I started to have crippling anxiety attacks. It was that bad.

What finally helped was time and the truth. I hired a PI, who got me reports from the police and the coroner, which was how I learned about the poor treatment my father received at the VA following his stroke. His whole body was gutted and he was in constant pain. Unable to work, and unable to get any of those charged with caring for him to listen to the problems he was having with chronic pain, he broke down. He threatened to jump off a building. He told people that he wished he were dead. Help did not arrive.

Finally, he got ahold of a handgun, and on the morning of the second Friday in February, the thirteenth, in 1976, he told his girl-friend at the time, a woman named Natalie, to go in the other room and call an ambulance, because he was in so much pain he needed to go to the hospital. Then, after she left the room, he took out his gun and killed himself. The police had to notify the next of kin, which would have been me and my younger brother, Jonathan. But my mother, stepfather, and grandmother answered the door and vowed never to tell anybody what really happened.

Over time, the truth of my father's death emboldened my hu-manity. As my back-and-forth with veterans proved, it made me tremendously empathetic on the campaign trail, and was some-thing of a surprise to those who were meeting me for the first time. People also loved it when I said I really wanted to win so I could get my sense of humor back and prove you can lead the nation and be funny. But my health at the time was no laughing matter. Thanks to a herniated disc pressing on nerves in my neck, I was in tremen-dous pain throughout the campaign, and every day it got worse.

At first, I kept the problem from everyone but Tim. Then, it was impossible to hide it. It turned my manageable migraines into crippling events, and I suffered from terrible spasms in my neck, numbness in my right hand, and excruciating pain every time I turned my head. I was popping Percocet like they were Pez and regularly calling time-outs to get spinal blocks and epidurals. The alarms finally went off when I asked my neurologist about mor-phine. At that point, Tim intervened.

"Should she be doing this and still running for office?" he asked.

My neurologist said no, I was risking permanent spinal damage if I continued rather than focus on taking care of myself. A solemn quiet engulfed us until Tim and I walked outside and got into the car.

"What do you think?" he asked.

"I think it's over," I said.

We went home, where I lay on the couch with our dogs wishing I didn't have to face any of this. Tim made calls to the campaign staff. The next day, they gathered around our dining room table, where I sat forlornly with my head bowed while Tim broke the news because I couldn't speak: My doctor wanted me to pull out of the campaign and prepare for surgery. When it was my turn to address these dedicated individuals, I just started sobbing.

"I can't do this anymore," I sobbed. "I can't move with this kind of pain. I have to listen to my doctor before I do permanent damage. And I've got to stop taking these pain meds."

Everyone was sweet and understanding. They all looked so devastated but still offered me nothing but hugs and support. I couldn't say the same for my Republican opponents. At the end of May, I officially dropped out of the congressional race, citing health reasons. Republicans fought to keep my name on the ballot rather than allow a substitute candidate, arguing that I hadn't "adequately proved that [I] would be physically unfit to serve in Congress." I thought they were despicable.

But the biggest battle I faced after withdrawing from the race was with myself. I truly thought I could win and, most important, help people who needed help. That was the reason I got into the race in the first place. I saw a need and wanted to make a difference in people's lives. And I believed I could. That was a terribly difficult idea to relinquish, especially in the summer of 2016, when I saw a shift taking place around me and in the country in general that I feared would ultimately result in more harm than help.

I don't mind when people hate me. But I have a serious problem if people feel I have let them down or if I fall short of expectations I have set for myself. I'm not comfortable creating disappointment. But I did know there was light at the end of the tunnel. I needed time to regroup and recover and get my life back on track. I thanked God I had that option. Except, as so many people discover when all they do is go, go, go, it wasn't an option. It was a necessity. My health, my marriage, and my family were more important than anything else.

I had to stop in order to move forward.

Whistle While You Work

I had already said goodbye to the bonnet. And the red gingham dress I wore back when I was portraying Laura Ingalls. And the black-and-white *Us* magazine photo of me pregnant with Dakota. And the wooden sign that said HALF-PINT. And my old Carman Allen boots. And Tim's autographed scripts from *thirty-something*. And his high school baseball jersey. Oh, and seven unopened bags of Morton salt.

It was goodbye, adios, adieu to those and more than two hundred other items from our shelves, closets, and kitchen pantry that comprised what was officially billed as the Melissa Gilbert & Timothy Busfield Estate Auction in Michigan. More than fifty-eight thousand people browsed the auction website, more than four hundred people registered to bid, and when the last gavel banged, we were sold *out*.

This was not a Kondo-inspired cleanse; it was more of a Swedish death cleaning. It was a purging of the past that had to happen. We needed to let go of things that we had treasured but really didn't need—not anymore. This was about figuring out what was essential for us and getting rid of anything that might distract from that or weigh us down with the past.

Six years earlier I had felt my heart open and given myself permission to follow that into a new marriage. This was about that next essential step: building a life together.

Tim and I weren't even at the auction. We were at our country house in the Catskills, giving it a fresh start. Well, not so much a fresh start as a very clean start.

It was January 2019, and not only had we gotten rid of our old shit, but we had also finally discarded and donated everything the previous owners had left behind when they left the premises. I was glad that was done. Every so often I still saw myself trying to capture the little mice who had scurried out of the mattress in the master bedroom so I could set them free outside, in what I suppose was my version of benevolent gentrification. But good riddance.

The few items of furniture and whatnot (i.e., the nudie magazine) that we saved were jammed into the kitchen while we scrubbed and bleached the place silly. Tim and I wore self-styled hazmat suits, goggles, and face masks. He concocted a mix of bleach and hydrogen peroxide specifically to mop down the ceilings, which were heavily mildewed and pretty gross.

We had feared that gunk might be black mold, but the guy who inspected the house said it was just mildew. I almost hugged him. We might have been the first couple ever to celebrate mildew with a high five.

This was completely different from past homes where I had lived. All of them had been in move-in condition and ready to be decorated—or in my case, overdecorated. In a way, this was like

Tim's and my relationship. We weren't scrubbing away our pasts as much as we were prepping a canvas on which we could paint a future together. This house was in need of TLC but its bones were solid and we saw the potential it offered.

It reminded me of the way we felt about each other when we met for brunch on our first date. Though both of us had been through some stuff, we were drawn to each other by the prospect that something interesting was going to happen if we let it.

Sometimes with relationships, remodels, and rehabs, you have to roll the dice in order to discover what the kids call *your best life*. Then, as was happening to me, you find out that the excitement of the process, of riding the river of possibilities, is your best life.

I mopped and scrubbed, listened to music, and enjoyed the various thoughts that shuffled through my head. At one point, I replayed a recent conversation with my mother. I had told her about an as-yet-unannounced documentary PBS was making about Laura Ingalls Wilder, the author of the *Little House on the Prairie* books, which were the source of my old TV series. In the early stages of production, they had inquired about interviewing me. My mother dismissed it, explaining that she preferred the seventies version with me and Michael Landon.

"They're completely different," I said.

"I don't want to know about the reality," she said. "I like the fantasy."

A lightbulb went off in my brain. That statement all by itself explained why she had never told me about my father's suicide. She wanted everything in her life—and, as a consequence, my life—to be sweet and pretty and gentle and beautiful. Nobody could be sad.

Nobody could be hurt. Nothing malicious could be said. None of this is a bad thing. Doesn't everyone want their children to grow up without pain and trauma? With my mom it was like a glaze. It was her glaze, the glaze she put over everything. The difference was that I was decidedly unglazed.

I needed to see things as they really were and then dig in even deeper to understand why. I was a student, a builder, a fixer, a searcher, a soldier in the battle for truth, which was, by the way, an absolutely maddening way to be in Donald Trump's Age of Alternative Facts.

We had a good time spending our days eradicating filth and grime. Tim already knew that I was willing to roll up my sleeves and dive into even the grossest projects, and I knew how handy he was, even though he disagreed and insisted that I was the man in the family. I did get a certain natural know-how with tools from my dad, whom I watched build furniture and fix things when I was a little girl. I'm also fearless. No one can ever accuse me of being a prissy princess. I'll try almost anything.

By mid-January, though, my body sent me a very clear message: *No mas*. It needed a break from the peeling, cleaning, and scrubbing. Back when we were still in Michigan, we had adopted a golden retriever from our dear friends the Smith family. They raised goldens, but they were also expecting their sixth kid, and when they heard we were looking for a dog, they introduced us to four-year-old Chevy, who had us with his first lick.

We were living out in the woods at the time and Tim wanted me to have a large dog with a big bark for when he was out of town. My tiny bulldog Josephine, who preferred to nestle in my lap or on the sofa, didn't cut it. But Chevy fit the bill perfectly. He was an adventurous free-roamer who spent hours exploring the woods on his own but somehow was always loping back when one or both of us wanted his company.

When we moved to New York City, Chevy was not thrilled. Unlike Josephine, he was not made for apartment living. Neither was he wired for daily walks on a leash. He missed being outside and free. It was more than hate. I could see the contempt in his eyes. *Apartment living in the city? You've got to be kidding me. This is not a life.*

Then one night while I was walking him, he saw a rat run out from one of the vents on the side of a brownstone. He took off, and the force of his lunging and then my trying to hold him back injured my shoulder. I waited months before I got it examined. Pictures revealed a badly torn rotator cuff. Surgery was inevitable.

But first things first. We found a new home in the country for Chevy with our friends Pete Benington and his wife, Kathy. They had a house on a lake, plenty of land, and children and grandchildren nearby, and they had recently put down their beloved twelve-year-old Lab. After much soul-searching, we proposed the idea. "Oh my God, are you kidding?" they said. " We already love Chevy!"

A year later, I was still avoiding surgery. I went from one play to another. Like any performer, I wasn't going to miss the chance to work. It's the ridiculousness of a "The show must go on" mentality. And I was continuing to put off surgery and live within the limitations of a bum shoulder until Tim and I were sterilizing the country house. After three days, I put down my mop and removed my goggles, which were filled with tears. My shoulder was throbbing. I walked over to Tim and leaned against him like a fallen tree.

"Timmy, I can't do any more," I said, speaking into his chest.

He consoled me with a tender hug.

Even that hurt.

Finally, the jig was up. On January 22, I flew to Michigan for surgery. The same doctor and friend, Laith Farjo, who had operated on Tim's shoulder repaired my shoulder. Afterward, I was in the most horrible pain I had ever experienced, childbirth included. I returned to New York in that condition three days later. It took six months for me to actually be able to put my hands on my hips.

We spent our first full night at the Cabbage, as I had taken to calling the place (a conflation of *cabin* and *cottage*), on February 2. We had to; our new kitchen stove was being delivered early the next morning. We set a mattress down in the middle of the living room. I was in a sling and couldn't do much. I applauded Tim (gently) as he built a fire in the brand-new wood-burning stove we had moved into the fireplace. To me, he was my very own Charles Ingalls. Soon, voilà: We had heat.

Though I was limited in how much I could help and do, we had a cozy first night until about two or three a.m. The fire was long extinguished and a cold draft from outside was coming in through the windows. I poked Tim, who was sound asleep.

"Timmy?"

I saw his eyes open in the dark.

"Yeah? Are you okay?" he said.

"Yes," I said.

"What's going on?"

"I have to pee."

"Okay."

"I need help getting outside," I said in the sweet little voice my mother used when she wanted a favor.

At the time, we did not have a working bathroom in the house. We had closed all the indoor plumbing for the winter. We had the old outhouse but it was still pretty nasty, so we had rented a porta-potty.

Tim helped slip on my Uggs and get a parka around me. Then he ushered me outside in the twentysomething-degree night, holding my hand and providing strong but gentle support to my wobbly body. When I came out, he was waiting for me, shivering but stalwart in his devotion to me, a prince in PJs, and I fell in love with him all over again.

We were a good team. In 2015, Tim was a producer-director on the ABC series *Secrets and Lies*, and I appeared in a handful of episodes. We shot in Wilmington, North Carolina. Tim's youngest son, Sam Busfield, was also part of the production, as the set's medic. A stint as a stuntman on the acclaimed series *Rescue Me* had inspired him to become an EMT. I loved watching Tim interact with his son and the look of pride that appeared on his face whenever he caught sight of Sam. His other son, Willy, had assisted him on numerous projects in the past and developed into one of the most sought-after cinematographers in the fashion world.

One Saturday, Tim and I and a few others from the *Secrets and Lies* cast and crew made a short film about a man who wants to leave his wife and daughter for another woman and tries to make that change all in the same day. Titled *One Smart Fellow*, we shot it in eight hours for about five hundred dollars. It won a slew of awards at film festivals. A year later, Tim and I collaborated again on a TV pilot called *Tenure*, which he had developed while teaching a class in TV production at Michigan State.

Then Tim's buddy Jeff Daniels proposed doing something similar together, and in 2018, we collaborated on *Guest Artist*, a feature film about an accomplished playwright who workshops his latest play at a theater in a small Michigan town. In the process, he is exposed as a broken-down, alcoholic asshole by an apprentice who gets a harsh lesson in hero worship. Tim directed, Jeff starred, and all three of us produced. I raised the money we needed for our budget, found our locations, and set up our production office before leaving to star in an Off-Broadway production of *The Dead, 1904* for the Irish Repertory Theatre in New York City.

Although I was only three weeks past my shoulder surgery when *Guest Artist* premiered at the Santa Barbara International Film Festival in February 2019, Tim and I flew there for the premiere. I wanted to be there as he walked the red carpet. It wasn't like the support he had given me when I needed to pee in the middle of the night, but I was a little obsessed with telling the world how stupidly talented he was. The man had depth, knowledge, wisdom, and a positivity that was inspiring to be around. He got things done. I adopted his motto: *One, two, three, GO!*

Of course, I reveled in the respect he showed me. Before Tim, I always felt like I had to make my own abilities and accomplishments smaller to allow the men I was with to feel confident, bigger, macho, and in control. Tim was different. Instead of feeling threatened by a strong, outspoken, capable woman, he encouraged me to meet each day fearlessly. He found it validating that I would want to be with him. For me, that was something new, wonderful, refreshing. I felt empowered to do and say anything. I was free to be myself. There was trust, and there was love.

And soon, if deliveries were on time, there would be a dishwasher, a refrigerator, and furniture.

If You Build It, Squirrels Will Come

The fridge and dishwasher came on time. The person who showed up to help me clean and scrub the rest of the kitchen because of my rehabbed shoulder also showed up at the agreed-upon time. And I gave kudos to the insurance inspector for doing the same. In the context of making the Cabbage livable, these were little things, of course, but I took them as positive signs that our relatively small and uncomplicated project was moving forward glitch-free and would continue that way as we demoed the kitchen, the bathroom, and the two bedrooms.

I was gravely mistaken. Before the Cabbage was ripped apart in April with an understanding that construction would be finished in time for us to have a July 4 celebration with family, Tim and I tried to anticipate the numerous issues we might find as walls and beams were taken down. Dry rot, mold, structural failure, electrical wiring, plumbing, etc. I don't remember everything but the list was comprehensive.

The one thing it didn't include was the fact that our contractor-carpenter Sal Bertolino's regular partner was injured and couldn't help. He brought in his girlfriend and another woman to help with the demolition, and they were fantastic, but not having his regular partner slowed things down exponentially.

Ultimately, our completion date was pushed back to November from July. Tim and I shrugged our shoulders and quoted the old CBS news anchor Walter Cronkite, who ended each night's broadcast by saying, "And that's the way it is." We were like everybody else in this situation—dependent on our crew. Two other factors also influenced the schedule: the weather and our budget. I knew plenty of people in Hollywood, contemporaries of mine, for whom money was no object. They had homes that resembled modern-art museums. They might as well have lived on another planet. For the most part, they did.

For us, money was an issue. We had used Tim's Directors Guild retirement to purchase the property and had reserved a slice of the remainder to deal with the renovations. Funds were limited. We had to be mindful of our expenses, which meant daily conversations about the most economical and least traumatic way to get the work done, while still achieving the vision we had for updating the Cabbage and making it our own.

This was just the reality of choosing art as a career instead of finance or law or computer programming or dentistry. It was also the reality of marrying for love instead of money. I know someone who only half-jokingly advises people to marry for money the first time and love the second. Tim and I were on round three, and while piles of money definitely can make life easier, we knew the only thing that gave a marriage any chance of working was love. The one thing that makes life full and meaningful is the only thing money can't buy.

So we researched vintage kitchens and did a deep dive into used barn wood, recycled hardwood, and aluminum siding, which was a design feature we wanted to use on one of the kitchen walls. One day, while scrolling through design sites online, I came across a feature on using recycled bowling alley wood for cabinets, counters, and furniture. I loved the look. The wood was sturdy and affordable and stylish. Tim liked it, too.

He picked up some boards at a place in Brooklyn and Sal turned them into gorgeous floating shelves in the kitchen and bathroom.

This was the first time I had ever decorated a house with a partner who insisted on sharing in all the decorating decisions. We chose everything together: flooring for the kitchen and bathroom, carpet for the rest of the house, doors, windows, sinks, faucets, knobs, cabinets, brackets, countertops, everything. It was quite nice and part of the healthy process of building a life together rather than trying to fit all the shit from our pasts into this new place.

Both of us were stymied in our search for a sofa, though. The living room had a slightly odd configuration that limited us in size and shape. It was kind of like finding clothes that fit and feel comfortable and look good after age fifty. You're willing to sacrifice more style than you would have in your twenties and thirties for the sake of comfort and fit. I mean, why would anyone wear skin-tight jeans or high heels after a certain age?

We wanted a sectional. A comfortable sectional. Determining the configuration became a wrestling match for us. We fell in love with the fun, funky sectionals at Roche Bobois, but we quickly fell out of love when we saw the price tag was fifteen thousand dollars at a minimum. I know it might seem like a trivial matter, a sofa, but most people only use a finite number of rooms in their home, no matter the size, and a good sofa is crucial. We intended our kitchen to be the gathering spot, and our living room with the sofa was the snuggle spot.

But until we had a sofa, it felt like we were setting sail without an anchor. The quest for the perfect sofa took up a lot of mental energy. Whenever we were in the city and passed a store with home furnishings, we darted inside for a look. Macy's. West Elm. Restoration Hardware. Used furniture stores. Tim and I texted and emailed pictures of sofas to each other. We measured and remeasured the space, as if it might have changed from one week or month to another. We were either determined problem solvers, borderline nuts, or both.

In the meantime, we bought a large brown recliner and a gray rocker, our Archie and Edith chairs. In early summer, we purchased premade kitchen cabinets but changed the knobs. We shopped for brackets for the freestanding shelves Sal made out of our reclaimed bowling alleys. In mid-August, we picked out our red kitchen countertops. A few weeks later, Tim and I googled generators; we needed one. We were at Home Depot and Lowe's so often we could have slipped on smocks and clipped on name tags, and people would have assumed we worked there.

This was all an exercise in *what do we need* versus *what do we want*. As someone who had previously subscribed to shopping therapy—my former business manager actually called me Spenderella—I liked this change. Tim and I had been making our lives smaller since moving from Michigan. Our watchword was *declutter*. But it didn't look like it from the outside. We had a big dumpster, burn barrels, a porta-potty, and multiple pallets of construction materials outside our little Cabbage.

The clutter and mess were temporary, but the animals who peeked at us from the edge of the woods or wandered into the yard, like the deer and the squirrels, must have had a few moments of head-scratching where they wondered what we were doing to their tranquil home. I'm sure we got terrible Yelp reviews from the mice we'd evicted.

Though we bought beds and bed frames, the Cabbage was still uninhabitable. Everything was piled up in the middle of the living room or filling the shed outside. We drove up and back on the weekends. Each time we turned off the two-lane road adjacent to our place and onto our driveway, the gravel crunching beneath our tires, we saw the property with fresh eyes. In April and May, the green on the trees was new, light, optimistic. In the summer, the woods were lush and thick. I imagined them busy with the business of those who lived there.

Some days were oppressively humid, which explained the mildew, but on most weekends I got out of the car, breathed in the clean country air, and had the childlike urge to run around the property, to run aimlessly, for fun, because I felt good. I knew exactly what had inspired novelist Henry James to write, "Summer afternoon— summer afternoon; to me those have always been the two most beautiful words in the English language."

Apparently he didn't have any comfy sweaters, because the fall brought its own magic: crisp air and foliage painted in blinding oranges, reds, and yellows. In October, we cleaned out the shed. I assembled a gigantic Quorum windmill-style ceiling fan by myself but needed help hanging it because it was heavy AF. Nevertheless, I still declared myself *prairie strong*!

By mid-November, enough of the work was completed for us to move in the bulk of our furniture. On the nineteenth, our washer and dryer were hooked up. The electricity, which we had rewired, worked! No overloads, no blown fuses. We also installed a propane tank and connected our generator in preparation for the power outages that we knew would eventually hit with the winter storms.

As always, we tried to think of all the eventualities that might cause us to have to hunker down there for an extended period, though not once did we consider a pandemic. That existential punch line was still a few months from being delivered.

Tim and I wanted to stay there a few days prior to Thanksgiving, and we would have if the plumbing and heating system had been fully installed, but work had understandably slowed as the holiday inched toward us. Tim, Michael, and I spent Thanksgiving in Michigan with Tim's surrogate family, the Beningtons. Barb, the warmhearted family matriarch who had ushered Tim through their front door and into their family's fold when he was a teen, was getting older, and we agreed it was important to spend time with her and my mother whenever we were able.

Afterward, we went to Ann Arbor for a fundraiser screening of *Guest Artist*. Then Tim flew to Sacramento to see his new grandbaby, Ruby, and then went on to LA to direct an episode of my sister's show, while Michael and I drove from Detroit to New York to begin settling into the Cabbage. On December 3, the heating system was good to go. Installation was finished. We started spending a night or two there, sometimes more, with the goal of tucking ourselves in tight by Christmas.

One afternoon a truck pulled up in front of our house. We weren't expecting anyone; I looked out the kitchen window. The truck was decorated with all sorts of doodads, metal figurines, and signs, including one that read IF YOU LOOT, WE SHOOT. It also had a Rudolph the Red-Nosed Reindeer head fastened to its grille. Kind of incongruous, until I saw the driver circle around his truck.

He was built like Hulk Hogan, with long white hair pulled back in a ponytail, a Fu Manchu mustache and goatee, more beads and dangling necklaces than Jack Sparrow, moccasins, a leather vest, feather earrings, and a pearl-handled revolver in a holster on his thigh. I clutched the counter and yelled for Tim.

"Um, honey . . . I think this is our neighbor!" I said.

That's exactly who it was, our next-door neighbor, Pete Traina, actor, stuntman, bodyguard, and sweetheart. He was proof that you can't judge a book by its cover. He arrived bearing welcome gifts, including a freshly baked apple pie. He also gave us herbs to boil to cleanse the spirit of the house, sage to smudge with, dried apples and other goodies, a book on the local history, and maps of the area. It was like the end of the first act of a *Little House* episode: Scary-looking guy shows up and turns out to be an angel in disguise.

In act 2, we met other neighbors—the squirrels. Like Pete, they were cute and furry, but they were not as nice. We heard them above our bedroom at night, and then we started hearing them in the walls and the ceiling during the daytime. There was more than one, and they were busy. We were unable to figure out how they were getting in. Clearly the squirrels were smarter than us, so we needed someone who could outsmart them if we were going to get rid of them.

I called city hall in Eldred, our nearest little town, and asked if they knew someone who dealt with wildlife and squirrels and all that. What I was trying to say was: *I need the phone number for the John Wick of rodent trapping and exclusion.* They introduced me to Fawn Schneider, head of the local animal control office and all-around fantastic human. She brought out tender traps that we put in the crawl spaces along the sides of the second-story loft. Two mornings later, we were awakened by the most gawd-awful screeching, a sound of horrendous distress and agitation.

In our sleepiness it took a moment for us to figure out the source of the noise. We learned fast that when squirrels get trapped, they run around like crazy, as would anyone. It reminded me of a line from John Carpenter's *The Thing*: "I don't know what's in there but it's weird and pissed off." This squirrel was beyond pissed. Fawn came over and let the squirrel go. This kept happening, with all the horrific sounds of a war going on overhead, until we finally located the holes outside the house and sealed them up. Busfields: 1; squirrels: 0!

Then the mice moved in. I guess they hadn't spoken to the squirrels. From the detective work we did, we discerned the first mouse ran down the inside of the fireplace and into the kitchen. At first, I was fine with that. It was just one mouse. I even left it little snacks by the fireplace, hoping it would eat those and stay out of the kitchen. But then we noticed the little critter had pals. There were two mice, then three, then five.

Tim went full-on serial mouse murderer, setting traps and issuing threats up into the fireplace. I suppose I was his willing recruit and cohort, but I wasn't quite as enthusiastic about the mouse murdering. One time, back in LA, I had found a baby squirrel. I showed Tim, who saw the look in my eyes, and before I could utter a word, he said, "No, you cannot keep the little baby squirrel."

"But—"

"Sorry, Halfpint."

We had done this dance before. Back in Michigan, we'd had a little tuxedoed cat named Charlie Chaplin. When I had gotten him in LA, he was a sweet, docile creature. Once he was in the Midwest, he changed from Charlie Chaplin to Charlie Manson. We would come home and find his prey laid out for our approval in the living room. One time it was a decapitated squirrel. Another time it was a bird. One day we were sitting in our backyard in Howell, enjoying a leisurely summer day, and Charlie, who had been heretofore resting on the grass, apparently asleep, suddenly leapt straight into the air and caught a bluebird midflight.

I once pulled a chipmunk from his jaws. To thank me, the little guy bit down on my finger and wouldn't let go. Unsure what to do, I drove one-handed to the nature center and showed them my hand with the chipmunk still lockjawed on my finger.

"Can you get this off?" I said, adding, "Without hurting either of us?"

Such incidents seemed to happen with an odd frequency. One

morning, while still in my nightgown, I was making tea in the kitchen when I heard a ruckus in the basement. I hurried downstairs and found Charlie Manson with a robin redbreast in his mouth. On closer inspection, I saw the bird was still alive. I also saw it was looking at me with an expression that clearly communicated it wanted me to help. I sprang into action and somehow freed the bird, who started to flap and squawk frantically.

Charlie looked like he was getting set to pounce again, so I grabbed the bird and shoved it up under my nightgown, which was weird, to say the least. I didn't know what the hell to do. Aware that I had to do something, I ran up the stairs and out the door to the end of our front walk, where I lifted up my nightgown and watched the bird fly out and away. I could only imagine what the neighbors must have thought was going on in my crotch region. Like, *Oh my God, she has a magic vagina!*

As Christmas approached, and with our critter problem solved, we switched our attention to the holiday. I was excited to celebrate at the Cabbage. We bought a tree at the fire station down the road from us. In Los Angeles, trees were trucked in from Oregon and Washington and cost two or three hundred dollars or more, depending on the size and shape. Ours was locally grown and cut, full and perfectly shaped, and only forty dollars.

Like most people, I was ticking off items on my holiday to-do list, and one day that took the two of us into Port Jervis, the closest facsimile to a city we had near us. The Home Depot was there. So were Price Chopper, Lowe's, and the bagel place I liked. It's about a three-hour train ride from Grand Central Station on the Metro-North line. We walked into the furniture store there, Royal Furniture, as we frequently did, just to confirm that we were never going to find a sofa, except this time we saw one that fit the bill. I don't know where it had been before, but it was there now, seemingly waiting for us, which was the way things seemed to happen, not when I wanted but when I needed.

Better still—and with apologies to Henry James—its display included two of the most wonderful words in the English language: *on sale*. It was eight hundred dollars.

"It is a pretty crappy gray color," I said.

"It is," Tim agreed.

"But I can cover it in really cool fabric from India and it will be great," I said.

I did exactly that, and it was great. We finally had our anchor as we sailed into Christmas.

Part Two

In the spring, at the end of the day, you should smell like dirt.

MARGARET ATWOOD

We'll Be Home for Christmas

Tim and I had our routines in the kitchen. He was the short-order chef in the morning and on weekends, and I, as the author of a bestselling cookbook, took charge of dinner on most weekdays. Tim characterized it as diner food in the a.m. and Michelin-worthy meals at night. Neither of us had any complaints. But for Christmas dinner, I eagerly handed the oven over to Tim, who made the turkey. But calling it a turkey doesn't do justice to this specialty of his that became our holiday tradition as soon as I tried it years ago.

It's that good—and we looked forward to it. We were at the Cabbage from Christmas through New Year's, the longest we had stayed yet. My son Michael joined us for the holiday, so it was the three of us there—actually there were four if you count Josephine, our French bulldog, who happily cuddled up in Michael's lap as soon as he arrived. The house was woodsy and cozy on its own and didn't need much decorating to give it a holiday feel, not that I had anything left after the auction. My Spode dishes and doodads were all gone. All I had saved was a box of Christmas tree ornaments.

Things like that were the real family jewels. The collection started back when I was a child and included ornaments my kids made in first grade, noodle frames with their photos inside. Once decked out with teeny colored lights, our treetop angel, and all the other adornments, the tree was festive and celebratory and home-spun, which was the way I liked it. I put some pine boughs and pinecones I found outside, as well as some apples and cinnamon sticks, on the fireplace mantel and added strings of white twinkle lights throughout the house.

As a final touch, I filled a couple of vases with dried hydrangeas from our yard and placed them in the living room and on the kitchen table. I had cut them late in the summer and early fall, and they had miraculously dried without shedding a single petal. I took a moment to admire both my and Mother Nature's work. When the thin winter sun shined through the windows, the dried flowers lit up, their beautiful dusty rose color illuminated like a still life painting and giving off good-mood vibes that brought the inside of the house together with the outside.

For me, Christmas was always joyful and fun. The same is true of Hanukkah. I grew up Jewish, and we celebrated both holidays. We celebrated everything—something I still do. Passover, Easter, Martin Luther King's birthday, National Hot Pastrami Sandwich Day, World *Star Wars* Day . . . you name a holiday and I'm all in. The Christmases of my childhood were always lovely and magical, with good food and lots of family, which I believe is the essence of the holiday: togetherness.

Back when I was married to Bruce and we were working on movies and TV series and money was rolling in, all pre–2007 recession, and we were in our seven-thousand-square-foot home in the Malibu hills, with high ceilings, we would buy a twenty-foot Christmas tree and throw huge, elaborate holiday parties. We flew in relatives. I started baking pies and making food days ahead of time. I set tables up all over the house. The flow of people and food was around the clock. It was like Christmas in Las Vegas. The gift-giving was insane. I made sure everyone was happy. And I had a helluva lot of fun myself.

My sister, Sara, uttered one of the funniest things I have ever heard one night when we were having Christmas dinner at my house. Bruce's parents and two of his siblings and their children were there. My family also came for dinner. I rented a few large round tables and set them up in two different rooms, expecting everyone to mix. But when it came time to sit down for dinner, the two families went in opposite directions: the Chicago Methodists in one room and the LA Jews in another.

During dinner, the conversation at our table focused on the ailments and diseases all of us thought we might have or could get in the future. The number of imaginary aches and pains and lumps all of us were suffering from was staggering. "Do you think the gentiles in the other room are having the same conversation that we're having right now?" I asked.

"No," my sister said. "They don't have to talk about it. They've actually had all of these ailments."

Tim and my and Michael's Cabbage Christmas, while smaller in scale, was no less fun or meaningful. It reminded me of all the *Little House on the Prairie* Christmas episodes rolled into one. We had all the great stuff about the holiday season—family, good food, games, warmth, laughter, and love. It was relaxed and easy. There was no pressure. For the three of us, it was all about being together, sharing the day, and snuggling in.

Outside, it was cold and snowy. The ground was blanketed with a thick layer of white and icicles plunged from our windows. On Christmas morning, we got up, ate something delicious that Tim whipped up, and got our stockings down from the fireplace. When I was growing up, we always got a Slinky and Silly Putty in ours. Tim put a spin on that tradition by putting Nerf guns in our stockings. This year he added big punching balls, the kind with heavy-duty rubber-band handles, and Michael and I had a fairly significant battle that ended with me rolling across the floor while he nailed me with his Nerf.

Much of the rest of the day was spent preparing dinner. Our kitchen felt like the Cheesecake Factory prepping for the evening rush. I made my pumpkin pie with a gingersnap crust. I had created this recipe about a decade before and made it every Christmas and Thanksgiving ever since. It's a perfect combination of fall flavors.

Gingersnap Pumpkin Pie

1½ cups gingersnap cookie
    crumbs
¼ cup granulated sugar
5 tablespoons butter, melted
1½ cups canned pumpkin
    (not pumpkin pie filling)

1 (12-ounce) can evaporated
    milk
¾ cup packed light brown
    sugar
2 large eggs
1 tablespoon cornstarch

1 teaspoon ground cinnamon   ¼ teaspoon ground nutmeg
1 teaspoon vanilla extract   ⅛ teaspoon salt

Preheat the oven to 325°F. Combine the cookie crumbs, granulated sugar, and butter in a 9-inch pie pan, pressing it into the
bottom and up the sides. Bake for 5 minutes. Let it cool completely.

Combine the pumpkin, milk, brown sugar, eggs, cornstarch,
cinnamon, vanilla, nutmeg, and salt in a large bowl. Whisk until combined. Pour the mixture into the cooled crust. Bake for
45 minutes to 1 hour, or until the pie is firm and has turned
slightly golden on top. Let it cool completely before serving.
Feel free to serve with cinnamon ice cream or fresh whipped
cream.

Tim then rolled up his sleeves and got to work on the turkey.
He started by preparing old-fashioned white-bread Pepperidge
Farm stuffing—moist and savory, just like the box says. Is it about
the turkey or the stuffing—which is more important? For us, I
think it might be stuffing. And both Tim and I are traditionalists.
We don't go for corn bread dressing, oyster and walnut stuffing,
sausage and apple dressing, wild rice, or any of the myriad varia-
tions that some people prefer. We are devout white-bread enthusi-
asts. As I think about it, too, it might be one of those questions
couples should ask before making any kind of long-term commitment.

Do you want children?

Are you religious?

Are you a dog or a cat person?

What about cookies—chocolate chip or oatmeal raisin?

Where do you want to spend holidays?

How do you express love?

Do you make the bed every day or leave it unmade?

If your mother calls while I am naked, will you feel compelled to answer? Or can you let her leave a message?

What kind of stuffing do you like with your turkey?

Tim and I were a perfect match. Only once did we hit a speed bump. Shortly after moving to New York, we ran into some old stuff. It reared its ugly head, which we recognized immediately and dealt with by seeing a wonderful marriage counselor, whose office was about fifteen blocks from our apartment. We saw her once a week for three or four months, and when we ran out of relationship stuff to talk about and began trading travel tips, we knew that we were finished.

It was time well spent. We had learned so much more about each other, we had built an even deeper level of trust and intimacy, and we emerged even closer than before. When it comes to making love work, you must be fearless, and we were.

Our commitment to longevity was behind Tim's Christmas gift to me: a weapon for defending myself if I was at the Cabbage while he was away for work and I needed to scare off an intruder, human or otherwise. Because we were vehemently against using a gun and my bad shoulder prevented me from shooting our bow and arrow, he got me a crossbow designed especially for ladies. It was pink camo, and it made me look like Rambo's badass little sister.

I don't think anyone in their right mind would approach me if I pointed that weapon at them. Despite the pink camo, it was huge, scary, and lethal-looking. I liked that it was very intentional. It took a minute to load the arrow, pull it back, and lock it into firing position. It meant I wasn't going to shoot myself in the foot. That said, we put up a target out back and I was able to hit the bull's-eye multiple times. I just couldn't do it quickly.

Then New Year's was behind us. It was 2020, and Tim and I returned to daily life in the city feeling rested and grateful for the simple little life we had created for ourselves in the country. When we bought the place, we wanted to create a getaway for rejuvenating and reconnecting with the basics, and each other, and it felt like we had done that.

A little more than a year had passed since we took possession, emptied out the previous owner's belongings, gave it a floor-to-ceiling scrubbing, and remodeled and updated. At each juncture, we asked what we *needed* to live there, really needed, as opposed to what we wanted, and what we found was that true joy and meaning came from the time we spent together working, sweating, freezing, planning, talking, discovering, eating, exploring, laughing, and falling into bed at the end of the day exhausted and in love.

You buy a house.

You build a home.

You fall in love.

You work to make love last.

Busy schedules limited our time in the country to weekends. Tim flew out to LA to promote his new ABC series *For Life*, and I stepped back into a calendar full of appointments, starting with my annual mammogram. As always, my sense that everything was fine was tinged by an undercurrent of what-if nervousness that served as a sobering jolt of reality. Time was limited. For everyone. What was I doing with mine? Was I wasting time? Using it wisely? Appreciating it? Was I doing what I was supposed to be doing at this time in my life?

I had asked these questions since I was a kid. However, now, in my fifties, I asked them with a new seriousness. When my mammogram came back all clear, I celebrated by going to ballet class. There's no better way to enjoy good news than to dance. Bad news, though, seemed to be in the air. First came a report that Terry Jones of Monty Python fame had passed away. I had met him many moons ago while shooting a movie in a remote part of China, where I was the lone American among a crew of Brits and Aussies and going through a hard time in my life.

Terry wandered onto our set from out of nowhere. As a major Monty Python fan, I immediately recognized him and freaked out. I still have no idea what Terry was doing in that part of China, but he spent the night carousing with all of us, singing Python songs and telling stories. It was the only time during that period when I forgot everything and laughed for hours on end. It was a lesson that we get through things. No matter how big the tears, they dry.

Or so I thought until I, along with the whole world, learned that Kobe Bryant had died in a helicopter crash in the mountains not too far from where I had once lived. In addition to the NBA legend, his thirteen-year-old daughter, Gianna, and seven others also perished in the accident. As I was walking down the street in the city, a news alert flashed on my phone. The moment I saw it, I stopped and literally gasped for air. My stomach was in my throat. I had no words, and still don't have any.

Like everyone else, I asked the obvious questions: Why, why did it happen, why him, why his daughter and the others on board, and how—how would their families go on? I sensed the emotional and existential cliff that Kobe's wife, Vanessa; their surviving children; and all their spouses and family members must have felt like they had stepped off. The horror of their loss and the sense of having no control was that dark room none of us want to enter.

Events of that magnitude have a way of stopping time. I remember getting back to our apartment and when I looked up I was staring at the picture of Meher Baba we have framed. He's seated on his bed, a garland of flowers around his neck and a smile creasing his face. Light radiates out from behind him. Every time I look at him, he seems to be telling me to be happy. *Don't worry. Be happy.*

Actually, his messages always boiled down to one thing: love. "When love is not at its height, it's always a mess."

Later, I watched the news and thought about how connected all of us are even if we don't always feel it, and also how alone we can feel and how incredibly fortunate those of us who find someone to share our life with are. Baba was right. It was love. My heart ached for the love that was lost in that accident.

I found myself with a need to be near Tim even more than usual. I wanted to go to the Cabbage and sit next to him on the sofa and cuddle up tight. As it happened, we'd had a new roof installed out at the Cabbage only the week before. Joe Duarte, the local contractor we used from Home Pro Exteriors, showed up with an army of workers and replaced the roof all in one day, new shingles, gutters, and all. It was a remarkable effort in teamwork; I felt a touch of Amish in the air.

I had never thought about our roof until we needed one. Then it was obvious why having a strong, sturdy one overhead was so essential. It offered protection from the cold and snow, the wind and rain, and the heat and humidity. It provided security from the outside world. It didn't leak. It hid us while we slept at night from alien spacecraft cruising the neighborhood. It completed the picture.

And in the wake of Kobe, I wanted to think of our roof as something that could shield us from calamity—everything except, perhaps, a meteor.

Then the meteor hit.

Praying for a Speedy, Uneventful Recovery

W̶e should think about what we are going to need if this gets really bad," Tim said.

I wondered why he had added the qualifier *if this gets really bad*. The past few days had been as crazy, weird, and scary as any time in my life. I had just been to the grocery store and seen with my own eyes empty shelves where only a few days before there had been an abundance of bottled water and toilet paper. Hand sanitizer was also gone, and Clorox disinfecting spray cleaner and wipes were nowhere to be found. The frozen food section was cleaned out, too.

Then Tom Hanks and Rita Wilson announced they had tested positive for COVID-19, as this new virus was being called, shortly after arriving in Australia, where Tom was filming a movie. They were quarantining in their hotel.

If that didn't drive home the point that every single one of us was vulnerable to this new plague, the pilot Tim was about to shoot for ABC was abruptly canceled. One day he was participating in a table read of the script with the cast of *thirtysomething(else)*, the much-anticipated sequel to the groundbreaking and beloved dramedy *thirtysomething*, on which he'd costarred in the eighties. The next day we were driving up to the Cabbage.

I had done my best to keep my fears at bay, but suddenly I was scared—and I hate being scared. I don't live in a place of fear. I have worked very hard over the years to get past my fears. Abandonment, which led to every bad decision I made in my life, was the biggest one I had gotten past, and the most recent one I'd conquered was my longtime fear of flying. I am still not crazy about spiders, but I deal with them.

The coronavirus was something I tried to ignore until that became impossible. I was slow to pay attention. I wasn't watching TV news at the time. It had become too loud and divisive and combative, so I read the news online every day as part of my morning routine. In early January, I saw mention of a pneumonia-causing virus that had reportedly made the jump from animals to humans in a wet market in China. Okay, I thought, here's a new terrible thing to put in my Gonna Keep an Eye on This One file.

This was followed by a report of the first case in Washington State, in a person who had recently moved from Wuhan, China. Then, in quick succession, the World Health Organization declared a global health emergency, our president banned travel to or from China, and then a public health emergency was declared in the US. Even as I read about it, I didn't take it seriously. I had no plans to travel to China, and I felt so bad for all the suffering in Italy. It still seemed esoteric and far away. I think a lot of people felt that way. It's the legacy, luxury, and privilege of living in a country separated from of the rest of the world by two giant oceans.

I had a feeling that we weren't hearing everything. We were living in such a weird world of "alternative facts," so it was hard to know what was true and easier to carry on as always rather than turn rigid from fright. In early February, we saw Matthew Bourne's *Swan Lake*. It was so stunningly beautiful, I started crying midway through the overture and didn't stop until I got into the cab to go home.

A few nights later, Tim had dinner with the cast of *For Life* to celebrate their first-season premiere. Another evening we went out with his *thirtysomething* costar and my old buddy Peter Horton, and the next day we drove out to the Cabbage. It had snowed the day before, and while the roads had been cleared, the grounds surrounding our little place were blanketed in white, a pristine white like I had never seen in my life. I was transfixed as I stared out the window the next morning, sipping my tea. The stillness of the snow on the ground and the way it was layered delicately on the posts of our wooden fence and the tree branches beyond gave me the sense of having stepped inside an Andrew Wyeth painting, where the moment captured is serene, quiet, still, and mesmerizing in its timeless beauty, but then, as you're drawn into the scene, you get the sense that something has happened—or is about to.

Tim and I both had the sense of calm before the storm, but not for the reasons that were soon to seem so obvious. He was excited about *thirtysomething(else)*, and I was excited for him to reconnect with the talented cast who'd helped change television when their show debuted in 1987. The series earned Tim an Emmy Award and three other Emmy nominations, along with friendships that deepened over time. I had never seen *thirtysomething* until Timmy and I started seeing each other. I got sick one week and binged the series.

I was absolutely blown away by the writing and the performances. I thought Tim's talent was next-level. I also think he's even better now than he was then, which is pretty damn amazing, but I understood the merits of the show and why it was iconic. His work on the new series gave me a chance to reconnect with Mel Harris, whom I had done a movie with ages ago, and Peter Horton, whom I was close with in the eighties. I also got to know Ken Olin and consequently his wife, Patty Wettig, and we had dinner with Polly Draper and her husband, Michael Wolff.

They were some of the most talented and accomplished actors on television ever, so respected in their own rights, and together they were truly something magical. I reveled in these new, wonderful friends and the positive creative energy and excitement that built around them as they prepared for the opportunity to do it again. The new scripts Tim let me secretly read were beyond brilliant. I went to Tim's wardrobe fitting and then lit out on my own to one of my very favorite shops in New York City, the Fine and Dandy Shop, a gentlemen's clothing store on West Forty-Ninth Street, where I picked out a bunch of natty accessories—hats, pins, socks, handkerchiefs, cuff links—that I thought would help him slip back into his character, Elliot Weston, albeit with an appropriately contemporary update.

Then everything came to a stop.

It happened quite suddenly. On February 19, I made an overnight trip to Sarasota, Florida, for a speaking engagement, and the following week I showed up in lower Manhattan for jury duty. When I heard Tom Hanks and Rita Wilson had tested positive for COVID-19, I posted a note on Instagram, praying they'd have a speedy, uneventful recovery. Then, in early March, a day after the table read for *thirtysomething(else)*, word went out to everyone that ABC was shutting down production before it began and getting all those who didn't live in New York City the hell out of Dodge.

We got in the car and drove out to the Cabbage. It was a Friday—Friday the thirteenth, as a matter of fact—and we didn't know if we would stay the weekend, the week, or longer. We didn't know anything other than things seemed to have taken a turn. I had a knot in my stomach. Each day seemed worse and bleaker than the previous, and the scariest part for me was knowing that we were not being told the truth. The virus was immediately politicized, which took it out of the realm of facts, and I sensed that, with the exception of Dr. Anthony Fauci, the administration had a bunch of incompetents in charge. They had been incompetent in every other way for the past three and a half years; I had no reason to believe they were all of a sudden going to be able to deal with a pandemic.

We listened to the radio and then turned on the TV news once we got to the house, and all the commentators were talking about worst-case scenarios, like outbreaks in meatpacking plants, interruptions to the food supply chain, and empty shelves in grocery stores. I was nervous for our kids and grandkids, who were scattered between New York, Austin, Sacramento, and Los Angeles, and my mother and sister and her kids, and Tim's sisters, brother, and all of their kids and grandkids . . .

My brain, fueled by anxiety, started to fire on all cylinders. What about people in hospitals? What about work? What about kids in schools? What were the precautions we needed to take to keep people safe? What did we need to do to keep ourselves safe? How were we going to help those who were more marginalized? What did we really know about this virus? How was it spreading? If it was just a little flu-like problem, like the Great Orange Turd claimed, why were so many people overseas dying from it?

I had questions—and fears.

I do much better when I know the facts. Even if it's bad, I want to know what's going on. I just want to know—and what I knew was that I didn't fucking know.

And neither did anyone else.

It seemed like everything was rapidly spinning out of control.

"I'm not hearing any cohesive advice coming from our leaders," I said to Tim. "It feels bad. It feels like we are all being left to go it alone."

I wiped a tear from my eye.

Tim was thinking. I could see the wheels turning in his head.

"We're going to be okay," he said.

"What do you mean?" I asked.

"We've got this place," he said. "We're pretty isolated. We have your crossbow. We have a lot of wild turkeys up here. We can hunt. We'll have food."

We googled how to dress a turkey. It was messy. I didn't want to go there, not yet anyway, and we didn't.

On Monday night, we were still at the Cabbage with no plans to leave. We hunkered down over the Scrabble board. "Social distancing," I wrote on Instagram. Almost immediately I learned that we weren't alone in this thing. "Same here in Norway," a fan wrote. "Schools, kindergartens . . . almost everything is closed. Take good care of each other." Another person added, "It's the same thing for us in France. We are confined for fifteen days." And still another wrote, "Greetings from Argentina. Staying home, too." My best friend Sandy Peckinpah added, "Bon courage à vous et votre famille."

If nothing else, it was clear that as alone and isolated and scared and confused as all of us might have felt, and while we attempted to figure out and consign ourselves to this new and very odd concept of social distancing, we were all in this together and closer than we realized. Tim and I had unknowingly spent the past year and a half getting ready for this moment. We had remade our little home in the country. Now we were going to hunker down in it.

For how long, we had no idea. We thought two weeks. Maybe a month. People were talking forty-five days max. Did they really know? What were they basing that on? We just wanted to do whatever we could to keep ourselves and everyone else healthy. We found out that Tim's daughter, Daisy, and her husband, Greg, were expecting their second child, a boy, that coming winter. That added to our worry for our beloved children and grandchildren. What was our world going to be like? How could we make it safer? Better?

We were grateful to have found this heavenly little patch of land in the country. It was as if we were starting out all over again, facing hardships—some known, some unforeseen—but that's life, and we had each other. Despite the circumstances, this was a good and fresh start, and Tim and I were ready. Ready to ask the questions. What did we need to survive? What did we have to do in order to thrive?

I thought of a line from the *Little House on the Prairie* pilot:

I knew there would be rivers to cross and hills to climb, and I was glad, for this is a fair land and I rejoiced that I would see it.

When the Going Got Weird

M y tooth broke.

I don't know how it happened. But after it did, I let loose with a few choice swear words, then inhaled and exhaled as deeply as possible and chalked the mishap up to one more thing beyond my control, like this COVID-19 thing.

Or this little Cabbage of ours. How was it that we had purchased it over a year ago, spent a year fixing it up, and then it was ready to shelter us just as everyone around the world went into self-quarantine, including us?

Some people would say it was the universe. Or that it was God. Tim and I called it a Baba thing. Whatever one wanted to call it, the whole situation very quickly became something all of us realized was destined for the history books.

But that didn't help my tooth. I may have absentmindedly knocked it a few times in the past on a teacup or a spoon, cracking it without being aware. Then I was talking one day and it just went *dink*. One of my top front veneers literally broke in half, like a brittle piece of china. The same thing had happened a few years before when I was visiting Tim in Nashville. One night we went to the movies and I popped off one of my veneers eating Skittles. (Talk about tasting the rainbow!) But it wasn't a problem. I immediately found the best cosmetic dentist in Nashville.

Not this time.

I had a wonderful dentist in the city, but New York was shut down and I had no idea who to turn to up here in the country. Tim got out his camera, and me, being the shameless creature I am, I said fine, mugged with my broken tooth, and posted it on Facebook, where the world could see my gleaming black gap.

I put it back together with Krazy Glue because I couldn't stand looking at myself. I looked like a hillbilly. The fix lasted a day.

You can DIY a lot of things but not dentistry.

I tried not to think about it. There were too many directions I could take such thoughts, none of them productive. As long as it didn't hurt, I was fine.

But my tongue didn't get the memo. In general, my tongue, like most people's tongues, did not have much to do all day other than lie around in my mouth. Once my tooth was broken, though, my tongue became obsessed with feeling the broken spot. It spent all day attempting to wedge itself into the gap or rubbing up against the sharp, pointy edge where my tooth had split in two. I could almost hear it talking to my other teeth, asking what the hell I had done—and when I was going to fix it. "This is entirely unacceptable. Does she know how she looks?"

I found the last open dentist's office near us in Monticello, New York. Though not an expert in cosmetic dentistry, the dentist removed what was left of my porcelain veneer and bonded my broken tooth. It was passable . . . not great but passable. Better than having a gap in my face. It was still stressful, though.

As long as I wasn't in pain, Tim kept me calm and maintained a healthy, realistic perspective. Wired not to panic in general, he saw there were other, bigger issues than my broken tooth. He returned from the grocery store the next day and announced in a voice muffled by the scarf wrapped around his masked face that people were freaking out. I waited for more information while he removed layers of cold-weather protection—gloves, scarf, jacket, hat, hoodie—as well as layers of virus protection: rubber gloves, then mask.

People were freaking out . . . hmmm . . . We were in the beginning stages of a pandemic . . . I had seen movies like this . . . Okay, I thought, people freaking out was to be expected.

But I could see in his expressive eyes this was different. I waited anxiously for him to tell me. Clearly, he had seen something bad, something so bad the best he could do was shake his head as if to say, "You're not going to believe what I saw out there."

"What?" I asked. "Was it the zombie apocalypse?"

"Close," he said. "There was no toilet paper."

I processed that information quickly. My brain works fast. Sometimes too fast for my own good. Why toilet paper? I didn't get it. Yes, life stunk now, but we had alternatives to TP. We had newspapers. We had showers. Human beings had been around for a couple hundred thousand years without anyone's squeezing the Charmin. Our ancestors went back six million years, and I was pretty sure that everyone had been pooping since then without going berserk about toilet paper. Toilet paper as we know it wasn't a must-have next to the commode until about the mid-1800s. What was the big friggin' deal suddenly about toilet paper? It didn't make sense. Why toilet paper instead of Tylenol? Or Pringles?

It must have been a control issue in reaction to a health crisis that was seemingly out of control. People are weird about poop. They don't want to know about it, see it, deal with it, or talk about it. However, if you're a parent, you spend the first five years of your kid's life up to your elbows in another person's poop. Then you're done. You don't mention it again. And you don't want to know about it—until you need diapers yourself and some poor soul is up to their elbows in your poop.

No doubt things were suddenly weird. In response, Tim and I ordered jigsaw puzzles. One way or the other, we were going to figure this out. We did eight puzzles by the end of March, including one that was a one-thousand-piece collage of bags of potato chips. We sat over them as if fitting the pieces together would reveal the secrets to a passage out of this *farkakte* situation. It didn't.

We segued to games—Battleship, Yahtzee, gin rummy, Uno, Trivial Pursuit, and backgammon, which was the game of choice in the Cabbage and the one that created the most intensity and fun when we played. Both of us are competitive, but not to the point where it's obnoxious or combustible in the way any game was when I was a kid and I erupted with volcanic anger if I lost to my brother, Jonathan. Tim and I played to have fun and could give each other a hard time without taking it personally.

From watching the news and reading about the pandemic, it

was apparent that the world's brightest scientists were working overtime to unravel the mystery while the world's biggest blowhards were spewing nonsense and politicizing our well-being as hospitals were filling up and grocery store shelves were emptying. Because we lived in a remote, rural area, where stores were small, their inventory smaller, and deliveries could take days or longer depending on the weather, and also because we heard several TV pundits talk about potential interruptions in the supply chain, it seemed prudent to prepare for a worst-case scenario, like how to survive long-term if necessary. That led us to purchase a giant outdoor freezer for our shed. We started to fill it with poultry, meats and fish, frozen vegetables, fruits, ready-made meals, orange juice, and other staples.

I also read up on additional foods we could freeze, like rice, cheese, butter, milk, egg whites, and bread, which we gradually added to the stash. I was like Granny on *The Beverly Hillbillies* stocking the root cellar. Tim and I didn't become survivalists, like John Goodman's character in *10 Cloverfield Lane*. But in the event our local stores ran out of food, or if going to the store became too risky, we were better prepared. We weren't going to starve.

In his 1979 book *The Great Shark Hunt: Strange Tales from a Strange Time*, gonzo journalist Hunter S. Thompson wrote, "When the going gets weird, the weird turn pro." Tim and I embraced that concept. I did something that I had never done before—I cleaned the house. I know the way that sounds, and I will cop to it. After all, I am someone who famously ratted myself out ages ago by admitting that when I had my first apartment in New York City, the dishes piled up so high in the sink that I saw only one way to re-solve that mess. I threw all of them out and bought an entirely new set. (#NotProudButHonest)

When I met Tim, I told him that not only did I not know how to clean a toilet, I was also an abject failure as a housekeeper. The pandemic changed that. Up till then we had a great housekeeper, Charity Iaconelli, who came every two weeks. She brought her kids, Tim would make everyone lunch, and it was like we all hung out. I absolutely adored her—and we needed her. But our collective fear of getting sick made it impossible for her to come clean any-more. She and we all felt that no one was going to leave either household until we knew what the hell we were dealing with. Henceforth, I said that I would clean the house.

My pronouncement was met with silence. On both ends.

But, with Tim's help, I quickly applied myself to the task of cleaning this wonderful place into which we had poured his sav-ings and our collective souls. It was an even greater challenge in the winter, as I discovered. Because even though we'd installed heat and insulation the previous summer, our little Cabbage was unable to fend off the cold when the outside temperature dropped and the wind threatened to huff and puff and blow the house down. We needed the extra boost of the wood-burning stove in the fireplace. But after we'd lit a few fires, though the flue drew perfectly, everything inside the house—and I mean everything—got covered with a thin layer of soot.

One day I woke up and had started cleaning the very sooty loft when I realized I hadn't yet put on my face cream. Very im-portant in the dryness of winter. So important that in the winter I splurge and use La Mer. I use a much less expensive brand the rest of the year. Anyway, I popped into the bathroom, grabbed a dollop of La Mer, and rubbed it all over my face, neck, and chest. I then continued cleaning. A little while later I caught a glimpse of myself in the mirrored vanity in our bedroom and gasped. I had smeared a mix of soot and La Mer all over my face. I now faced a horrible dilemma: wash off this very expensive mud mask I'd created or let it all soak into my skin. I decided on a hybrid and wiped most of the soot off with a cotton pad and let the rest soak in. Hey . . . it was LA MER! That shit is expensive!!

Soot or no soot, the fire was incredibly important for us. The pride I took in the dancing flame and orange embers went beyond the warmth it provided. Why I felt this way had little to do with the pandemic, though our self-quarantine certainly did add context. It was what it represented—not the typical frights of destruction and hell but rather what I saw in it: the heat of passion, desire, independence, and rebirth. Fire was light. It was change. It was power. It was me. I had always been the fiery redhead, and now my natural hair color was duller and streaked with gray, and you know what? I was okay with that. It was me.

And inevitable. I remembered being in Screen Actors Guild board meetings and Tess Harper raising her hand for a point of personal privilege and asking whether it was hot in the room or she was having a "personal summer." I had no idea what she meant until I started carrying a little electric fan around with me. I went to the doctor, who might as well have said, "You idiot. You're in menopause." I was offered all kinds of fixes—hormone replacement, herbal supplements, etc. All these things that might trick various parts of me into feeling and looking young, except their side effects raised the chance of breast cancer, ovarian cancer, tumors, blood clots, heart attacks, bloating, headaches, mood changes, and other fun stuff.

Everybody has their own issues and reasons for deciding what they will and won't take. Do I want to sit in front of a 20x magnifying mirror plucking whiskers from my chin in the morning? No. But I'll do it. To me, the issue is not so much menopause as it is aging in general. What do you think our grandmothers meant when they talked about "the change"? That was code for what we now describe as "WTF happened to my hair, my face, my body, my . . . ?"

Hello! I was experiencing *the friggin' change*.

I was a super-shiny redhead, almost like a neon light, who walked into a bar or restaurant and could feel heads turn, especially men's, and now I am not the younger woman, not the siren, not the hot commodity that stops the clock. That's a change.

On the flip side, I am so much more comfortable in my own skin. That's also a change, a welcome one that I earned.

And get this: As I have become sort of invisible, I feel like I have also become more of a secret weapon. I don't feel aging is a bad thing as much as it's a dire underestimation of what's still possible, of who I am. I am content with what my body is doing. I still look cute in overalls, which have become my daily uniform and which are very forgiving. I deal with the inevitability of change, even during the shitstorm we were in then.

It's all part of seeing life as a graceful transition from one phase to another. It's part of being a grounded, calm person.

Not that I am above or beyond screaming with delight. Such was the case when Tim returned from the store one day. I wasn't going out. He was our sentry, our all-in-one search and rescue. Excited, he wanted to show me the bags he had brought home but set outside because at that point we weren't bringing anything inside until it had been disinfected and wiped down with Lysol wipes we had found on Amazon for something stupid like thirty dollars a box.

I followed him outside, where he didn't just show me but provided a personal introduction to each item. "Beans!" he said. "Cans of beans and peas and fruit cocktail! And coffee! And soup! And canned tuna! Ramen! Kraft mac 'n' cheese! It's a miracle!!" My eyes bulged out of my head like I was some crazy Warner Bros. cartoon. I'm surprised the sound "ayooogah" didn't explode from my brain. I don't know if everyone was this crazy, but each of these items was suddenly more meaningful than ever, and finding them made us a little nutso. Every box from the UPS guys was a treasure trove: a bag of garlic bulbs, Lysol wipes, a digital thermometer, flour, a new jigsaw puzzle, and the Birkin bag of the pandemic— THE N95 MASK!!! Tim once called me from the dollar store after finding tiny Smurf-shaped bottles of hand sanitizer in a bin of kids' toys. You'd have thought he'd discovered uranium.

At the end of March, Tim found toilet paper on Amazon. Once again, he was the victor in this nationwide scavenger hunt. He yelled out, "Got it!" as if clicking on the Buy Now button was delivering us the six winning numbers in the Mega Millions lotto. We were, in fact, suddenly *butt rich*—or so we thought. A few days later, the box arrived from China. We tore it open, excited to be in possession of this holy grail of tushy wiping. But our smiles suddenly disappeared, the ecstatic delight of instant wealth literally vaporized, as we found ourselves looking at a box full of the cutest rolls of miniature toilet paper ever made. If Barbie pooped, she would have had these rolls in her bathroom.

We laughed.

Greed is greed and need is need, and never the twain shall meet.

We were good.

The next morning I made a delicious breakfast salad consisting of arugula, cherry tomatoes, chopped cucumber, scallions, crumbled turkey bacon, and oil-and-vinegar dressing. I finished it with two perfectly poached eggs speckled with salt and pepper. It was gorgeous. It would have cost forty-five dollars at a spa. It radiated health, and I intended to eat healthy for however long this quarantine lasted. But damn it, what I really wanted was a plateful of mashed potatoes.

The Five Stages of Cooking

Soon nearly everything in the house was labeled. Dresser drawers were marked SOCKS, BRAS, UNDERWEAR. The cabinet above the washer and dryer bore the white-and-black block letters DETERGENT, BLEACH, and FABRIC SOFTENER. Inside the freezer was a marvel of organizational commitment, containers neatly stacked and clearly labeled SAUSAGE GRAVY, CHICKEN GRAVY, SAUSAGE & PEPPERS, MAC & CHEESE, CHICKEN SOUP, and so on.

Then I tackled Tim's camera and sound equipment. SOUND CABLES, LENSES, BATTERIES, LIGHTBULBS, CAMERA CABLES.

A little obsessive? Sure. But so what. I didn't want to be the only one in the house who was organized. Neither did I want to be the one yelling, "That's doesn't go in there." But the real story, the nitty-gritty, was this: I had been having a flirtation with my digital label maker for a couple years. I just hadn't had the time to devote to the relationship. Once we were locked down, though, things changed. I needed to do something remotely constructive besides eating carbs, and I decided to organize everything.

It was my way of coping while I got my pandemic sea legs. I have always done this. I can't recall how many times I have cleaned out my junk drawer or reorganized tool chests, putting all the pliers together, bundling the screwdrivers, and sorting nails and screws. I did this every few months under the best of circumstances. My therapist said I was someone who needed to try to control my environment when everything else seemed out of control.

Duh.

I grew up in a house with little to no real organization. If I were to open my mom's makeup drawer today, it's a pretty good bet that I might find products in there kind of mushed together, some dating back to the early sixties, which is scary, since she has moved a few times since then. Except for knowing when I had to get up, go to work, and do my homework, everything else was a bit of a chaotic free-for-all, and beneath the surface, there was some untruthful, secretive stuff going on, which instilled in me a sense of uncertainty about what was coming next. Consequently, I became a bit of a control freak.

These early days and weeks of the pandemic—described by the *New York Times* as "profoundly chaotic and unsettling"—exacerbated my quest for control. I don't think I was alone. Nor do I think this was anything new. Trying to bring order to chaos seems like a natural human response to the mystery of existence, something humans have been doing forever. Not everyone reacted like me, but as the coronavirus spun out of control, everyone was trying to make sense of what was going on and figure out what to do. I made labels.

I also cooked. We weren't going anywhere. I wasn't going to be on camera anytime soon. It was cold outside. And I was a little unhappy, and a little uncomfortable—an evil combination of things that made me crave comfort food. I opened up my 2014 cookbook, *My Prairie Cookbook: Memories and Frontier Food from My Little House to Yours*, and I grinned the way one does when they hit the mother lode of feel-good food.

Aha, I said to myself, this is where all the mouthwatering, high-calorie, carb-laden meals are located.

Inspired and suddenly starving, I set out to *Julie & Julia* my way through the recipes: macaroni and cheese, pasta with mushrooms, shepherd's pie, fried chicken, spaghetti carbonara, mashed potatoes, creamed spinach with bacon and shallots . . . Every bite was like getting a hug from Mom. And speaking of Mom, my mother was doing the same thing on the West Coast. When I checked in with her, she was making my favorites from childhood and her favorites from the *Colorado Cache Cookbook*, like spaghetti pie.

Spaghetti pie was essentially a casserole. I knew it well. I literally moaned when she mentioned it—partly from the pleasurable memory of the mozzarella, sour cream, Italian sausage, onions, tomato paste, and butter baked in a cooked spaghetti, egg, and Parmesan crust, and partly because I wished I had been there to help her eat it, which I mentioned to my mom. A few days later, the recipe showed up in my mail. God bless her, I thought as Tim and I sat down to our own dish of spaghetti pie.

Spaghetti Pie

(Courtesy of the *Colorado Cache Cookbook*)

6 ounces spaghetti	1 pound Italian sausage
2 eggs, beaten	1 (6-ounce) can tomato paste
¼ cup grated Parmesan cheese	1 cup water
2 tablespoons butter	4 ounces mozzarella cheese,
⅓ cup chopped onion	sliced
1 cup sour cream	

Preheat the oven to 350°F. Break the spaghetti in half and cook in boiling salted water according to the package instructions until done. Drain. While still warm, combine the spaghetti with the eggs and Parmesan. Pour into a well-greased 10-inch pie plate and pat the mixture over the bottom and up the sides with a spoon.

Melt the butter in a skillet, add the onion, and sauté until limp. Stir in the sour cream and spoon the mixture over the spaghetti.

Remove the sausage casings and discard. Crumble the sausage and cook it in the skillet until done. Drain. Add the tomato paste and water. Simmer 10 minutes. Spoon the sausage mixture on top of the sour cream and onion mixture. Bake for 25 minutes. Arrange the mozzarella on top and return to the oven until the cheese melts.

Note: This freezes well, so double the recipe and freeze a pie for later.

My friends were also spending hours in their kitchens. We started exchanging recipes. Longtime pals who were die-hard vegans or plant-based and keto fanatics were now eating Swedish meatballs and creamed chipped beef on toast. Everyone, it seemed, had climbed aboard the comfort food bandwagon at the same time. Soon Tim and I were eating peanut butter and jelly sandwiches, grilled cheese, and cheeseburgers for lunch. We had talked about living a full life under quarantine. But not this kind of full.

I look back on this as a period of growth. Others called it the COVID nineteen—as in the nineteen pounds everybody seemed to gain. I learned to open up the pantry and cook with whatever was on the shelves. Before the pandemic, I was never the kind of cook who opened up the cupboard and said, "Look, bread crumbs, olive oil, peanut butter, quince paste, and a can of peas. I can make a fantastic Mediterranean timbale." No, I planned our meals, shopped for fresh ingredients, and cooked as if I were chasing a Michelin star.

But necessity changed me. One day I opened the pantry and saw a can of sardines. I didn't know where they had come from. I didn't remember buying them. And if I had—or if Tim had—I could not imagine why. But there they were. I opened my *New York Times* cooking app, plugged in *sardines*, and up popped a recipe for sardine toast. I read the ingredients. I had an onion, some garlic, tomatoes, sugar, salt, pepper, and olive oil. And I had bread in the freezer.

Perfect, I thought. It was a complete meal, with protein, veggies, and a little bit of carbs. *Et voilà*—sardine toasts! Which were delicious, by the way.

It became like a game. The next day I looked in the pantry and found a can of refried beans. From the dining room, where Tim was working on a script, he overheard me say, "Huh, refried beans. What can I do with those?"

"Burritos!" he yelled instantly, as if he had hit his buzzer and was shouting out an answer on a game show.

"I don't know how to make burritos," I said.

"I'll make you a burrito," he said.

Food was our way of coping. By the middle of April, I realized that we were cooking our way through Elisabeth Kübler-Ross's five stages of grief as we mourned our lost freedom to travel and socialize. We moved swiftly past denial, anger, and bargaining. Depression was a different matter. One afternoon, while Tim and I were watching the news, I just burst into tears. When Tim asked what was wrong, I said, "I miss my mom. I want to see my mom."

All the things that were going on winnowed down to the most essential thing that brought comfort and security, and for me, that was my mom. All of a sudden I missed her tickling my arm the way she did when I was a little girl. I was in my fifties now and I hadn't thought of that for years, even decades. I am surprised I didn't start sucking my thumb again.

Similarly, one day I turned to Tim and told him that I was missing my dad. Badly. Like so bad I could feel an ache in my heart.

"He would know what to do," I said. "Not that you don't know. Or that I don't know. But he would *really* know."

Acceptance, the last of the five stages, came in waves, starting with the bologna sandwich that I made myself one day for lunch. I hated this sandwich when I was a kid because everybody else brought fancy stuff for lunch and I had my sad slices of bologna with mayonnaise on white bread. Now it couldn't be beat. Then we got a milkshake maker. Tim was the milkshake man, and after every meal, there was a malt. And then he came home with a deep fryer. We needed it, he said, to go with the griddle we already had.

Well, I saw what was going on. Unable to go out to a restaurant, we brought the restaurant to us by turning our kitchen into the local diner. One day he made donuts. Days later, not to be out-done (or out-eaten), I found a recipe for beignets from Café du Monde. With a deep fryer, they were perfection. There was just one problem. The recipe made two dozen, and so Tim and I ate six each before waving the white flag.

I created a menu board and updated it daily with whatever we were making for dinner plus an inspirational quote. Everybody I followed on social media seemed to be showing off their sourdough starters and pasta dishes. I thought it would be fun and entertaining and perhaps a little provocative to share some of the thoughts Tim and I had, tiny windows into our sense of humor and our souls.

Self-Quarantine
Day 33
Pan-Seared Halibut, Green Beans Almondine
"Don't Worry, Be Happy"
—Meher Baba

Self-Quarantine
Day 35
Pan-Seared Ribeye, Hash Browns, Roasted Broccoli
"The Other Day I . . . Oh Wait, That Wasn't Me"
—Steven Wright

Self-Quarantine

Day 39

Shepherd's Pie & Spinach Salad with Bacon Vinaigrette

"Here, Kitty Kitty . . ."

—The First One to Die in Every Horror Film Ever

Self-Quarantine

Day 40

Leftovers

"We Could Never Learn to Be Brave and Patient If There Were Only Joy in the World"

—Helen Keller

Self-Quarantine

Day 44

Ginger Soy Salmon, Roasted Asparagus, Jasmine Rice

"Be Kind Whenever Possible—It Is Always Possible"

—Dalai Lama XIV

All of it may have been an extension of my label making.

We were adapting, I think—adapting to the unknown, to stress, to fear, to constant concern for our family, friends, and neighbors— and hoping, indeed believing, that if we survived, if we wore our masks, washed our hands, socially distanced, and prayed for scientists to come up with a vaccine, we might come out of this better, stronger, wiser (and heavier). But while we were locked in, we were determined to make the best of it.

I started taking Italian lessons. (One of the dumb things I did.)

I tried learning the ukulele. (It didn't stick.) I took up mosaicking bits of broken china on old vases. (Meh.) After seeing Sharon Stone hold up a beautiful paint-by-numbers picture she had made, I ordered my own kit and began work on my own masterpieces. I did several Monets. They were my favorites. Call me Monissa, I declared. In the meantime, Tim picked up the guitar, and soon he was writing songs. I marveled at his gifts.

And his Zen. Tim honestly believed that everything was meant to happen for a reason. Said reason may not have been immediately apparent, he said, but it eventually and without fail would reveal itself. Patience was not just a virtue, it was a requirement. I took his outlook to heart and appreciated having a partner who knew how to set a course through these uncertain times. I allowed myself those quiet moments of loss and sadness and fear and uncertainty when they came, and I let myself believe that good things were going to come out of this for all of us.

Connecting with my kids helped buoy my spirit. So did the quiet at night, the sound of snow falling, and the wind singing in the treetops. I could feel the depth of the night and the distance of the stars. This was eternity—everything that had happened before and everything that was going to happen later—reminding me of my humble place in this world and enormous responsibility because of it. I thought of how short our time here is and how important it is not to waste it. Tim and I celebrated our seventh wedding anniversary, and I went to bed feeling blessed. I thought of my own humanity and the connection it provided to billions of others who shared similar feelings of love, kindness, and hope.

I tried to make sense of something so big and overwhelming that it seemed to have stopped time and slowed our full-speed-ahead lives to a crawl, and I concluded that we were being tested—life had abruptly been pared to the basics so we could see what was truly important. This was the reason we were all involved in cooking and crafts, missing family and friends, doing puzzles, going for hikes, and hoarding toilet paper. We were figuring out what really mattered, what we needed as human beings, as opposed to what we wanted.

Tim was right, I thought. Everything happened for a reason. But as someone who began life as Baby Girl Darlington and became Melissa Gilbert when my parents adopted me the day after I was born, I needed no convincing that explanations came as bread crumbs on the long trail of one's life. There were reasons Tim and I had found a place in the country, fixed it up, and chosen to spend the lockdown there. Some I knew, some I didn't, and some I was beginning to sense. Ours were a home remade and lives rediscovered. It was all part of what I began to see as our graceful evolution.

Knowing this helped me feel less frightened and more in control. One morning I woke up and thought, What can I do to help somebody else today? I decided to give blood. I had heard on the news that blood donations were down. I logged on to the Red Cross website and sure enough, they needed blood. The pandemic had scared everyone off. Nobody was giving blood, which is such an essential need and such a simple thing to donate.

Tim and I discussed it, because we were being told not to go outside and touch anything or breathe near anyone, and puncturing your skin to get into a vein in a room where the virus could be lurking might not be such a sensible thing to do. But the Red Cross website was very reassuring with all their precautions. Indeed, once I was there, the process was very organized and safe and easy. With a mask on, no one recognized me. At the registration table, I gave my name.

"Melissa Gilbert—like the *Little House on the Prairie* Melissa Gilbert?" the woman checking me in asked.

"Yes, just like her," I said.

"Wait a minute . . . you sound just like her," said the woman.

"That's 'cause I am her," I said.

The whole thing took about an hour. Afterward, I had my juice and cookies and posed for pictures with the volunteers and nurses, in our masks. They thanked me. I thanked them. Pandemic or not, we were all in this together.

Self-Quarantine

Day 49

"Service to Others Is the Rent We Pay for Our Room Here on Earth."

—Muhammad Ali

Doing the Funky Chicken

Like me with *thirtysomething*, Tim didn't get around to watching *Little House on the Prairie* until well into our marriage. Once he dove in, he was more than hooked. He was fascinated. By everything, every little detail, and especially by Michael Landon, the series star, creator, executive producer, writer, and director.

It made sense. Tim was himself an insanely prolific and talented producer, director, actor, writer, and professor who couldn't learn enough about the creative process.

One day he was peppering me with questions about the origins of the series, starting with my audition and screen test as a nine-year-old and the instant connection I had with Michael. We talked about the two-hour movie that served as a pilot and then shooting the initial season on our *Little House* set at the Big Sky Movie Ranch in Simi Valley. I still had the very first script with my lines underlined in red crayon—my technique at the time.

I was off and running and ready for this adventure, I said, while reminding my husband that I was only nine when the show started production in 1974, and what I remembered exciting me more than anything were the costumes. They were built from the bottom up, I said. We had authentic high-button boots. I got to learn how to use a buttonhook, which I thought was cool, though later on that buttonhook got to be a royal pain.

"But everything was really authentic," I said. "We had pantaloons and—"

"What is a pantaloon?" he interrupted.

They were the prairie equivalent of underwear, I explained, comparing them to bloomers and granny panties. We also had cotton tights and garters, petticoats, dresses, pinafores, and sunbonnets.

"Even as a kid," I said, "without a real professional process for getting into character, I looked in the mirror when I put on that costume for the first time and I went, Okay, there she is. I know who this is."

I felt the same way as a fifty-six-year-old when Tim and I brought baby chickens home. Yes, chickens—tiny baby hens, or maybe roosters. They were too young for us to know the mix we had, but I took one look at them huddled together in the box that was their new home and I knew raising these chicks was a role waiting for me.

I had no doubt. I was a motherclucker.

We had been talking about having chickens at the Cabbage for the longest time. Also horses, goats, and even a pig. We had fourteen acres. For two people who had been living comfortably in a small apartment in New York City, that land looked like a spread of endless possibilities. Prior to the pandemic, we resisted getting animals because we would have needed a caretaker, but once we decamped to the Catskills, we reopened discussions. Then food-stuffs became scarce and unpredictable, and Tim and I mulled different scenarios.

Though we sounded like we were playing survivalists in an improv scene, we tried to be practical. Cows and pigs were out. Chickens were not.

"We have to get the chickens," I said. "If this gets worse, who knows what kind of food is going to be available."

Tim agreed. "Even if it doesn't get worse, it's a smart thing for us to have in case something else happens later on and we need to be fully independent."

We were convinced independence and preparedness were keys to managing the future. We had our generator. We had the propane tank. We had our well. We also had our outside freezer. We laughingly nixed the idea of building a bomb shelter as too crazy, and we weren't buying any guns. But we did have the crossbow Tim got me for Christmas. He did some more googling on how to shoot and dress a turkey, because we did have a large population of wild turkeys in the area, and that could sustain us if we devolved to a place where every day was turkey day.

But chickens seemed easier and doable and more fun for the time being than stalking wild turkeys. We researched what was entailed in raising chicks: how long they needed to stay inside and be kept warm until they could live outside (eight to ten weeks); what kind of space they needed outdoors; how long until they laid eggs (about four and a half months); and so on. The two of us liked creating all sorts of things. Tim had built sets in his theater companies. He loved nothing more than bringing an idea to life. Getting chickens was our next production.

We bought all the supplies—a Brinsea brooder, pine shavings, feeders, waterers, food, probiotics, and treats. We took a large plastic tub, and Tim cut out the center of the lid and stapled chicken wire to it so the chickens would have a roomy, warm place to live in a corner of our kitchen. All we needed was the chicks. But the craziest thing happened—we couldn't find chicks.

It was the beginning of May, the sweet spot of spring, yet snow was still falling. Outside, the white stuff fell in my favorite big, chunky flakes. The view from the window was beautiful and serene, as if this was one last nap before the air warmed, the snow melted, and everything bloomed. I couldn't wait. Tim was on the computer searching for chickens.

"I can't find any," he said. "They're on back order until July or August."

It was true. Everyone across America had the same idea at the same time. Chickens became the toilet paper of the spring.

Finally, we found a chicken breeder in upper Pennsylvania who had chicks ready to go. When you buy chicks, either you get them already sexed, so you know what you're getting, or you get what's called a straight run—day-old chicks too young to separate by sex—and take your chances. All he had available was a straight run of Deathlayers, a German breed that dated back hundreds of years. Many breeds of chicken go through menopause and stop laying eggs a couple of years before they die. These gals produced eggs right up until their final days.

"Deathlayers—sounds like a motorcycle gang or a goth band," I said to Tim as we drove to the Pennsylvania farm.

We got nine chicks and brought them back to the Cabbage in a little box that I held in my lap, cooing at their cuteness the entire way. Nothing about them was scary or intimidating. They were like large cotton balls with tiny feet. Sadly, one died later that night, despite my nurse-like efforts to keep it alive, but the others huddled together in their bin and kept each other warm and healthy. We named most of them after the Little Rascals: Porky, Buckwheat, Spanky, Darla, Alfalfa, Woim, and Stymie. The other two we called Puffy (because he or she had a puffy chest) and Dr. Fauci, aka Biggie, as he or she was the biggest of them all.

As they made themselves at home, they brought out my maternal instincts, which were never too far beneath the surface, anyway. Just in time for Mother's Day!

Self-Quarantine
Day 57

The Mother is everything.

She is our consolation in sorrow, our hope in misery, and our strength in weakness.

She is the source of love, mercy, sympathy, and forgiveness.

He who loses his mother loses a pure
soul who blesses and guards him
constantly.
—Kahlil Gibran

The tiny babies needed lots of care and nurturing. I checked their water and made sure they were fed. Every morning we would have what I called "lovely lady time," where I would put on classical music for them and wipe each of their little butts and daub them with olive oil to keep them clean. They could get sick if their butts got crusty and clogged. They also got a little extra TLC. If Tim got up early, he put two or three of them into bed with me. Later in the day we had playtime with them on the living room floor. And at night, they settled under their brooder in a little ball of fluffy feathers that made them so stinkin' cute.

Before we got our chicks, we had been talking and reading about building a chicken coop. I wondered where we could purchase one. I read about high-quality Amish coops. I wondered whether if we bought one of those it would also come with a bunch of Amish guys—Jeremiah, John, Amos, and Levi—to put it up. We could host a chicken coop raising.

Alas, although the Amish chicken coops I saw online were gorgeous, they were also very pricey, and Tim and I were on a DIY budget. We were the aspiring Chip and Joanna Gaines of the Catskills. We researched coop plans. We looked into where in the yard it was going to go, what kind of fencing we needed, and what we needed to do to protect our chickens from predators who lurked above- and belowground—hawks and eagles, turkey vultures, bobcats, coyotes, raccoons, and snakes, among others.

It was like the sidewalks of New York City in that way, except the bad guys, who wore fur and feathers, weren't actually bad guys. As the song in *Annie Get Your Gun* goes, they were just doing what comes naturally. Living out in the woods, we had to respect that— and do our best to protect our fine feathered friends.

Which we went to great lengths to do. Tim drew up plans while I looked into the best materials to use. He consulted with me and compared my recommendations with those he heard from the guys he watched on how-to YouTube channels. I referred to those guys as his boyfriends, because all I heard him talk about was this guy or that guy on YouTube. It was as if he knew them, and I suppose he did to an extent. He spent enough time with them.

Eventually, with our first batch of chicks living in the kitchen, we ordered a coop online that proved way too small after seeing it in person. It reminded me of the Stonehenge replica in *This Is Spinal Tap*. But hey, live and learn. Intent on not wasting any more time, we bit the bullet and ordered one of the larger, more expensive Amish coops. More like a multistory condo than a coop, it was big enough for me to climb inside, which I did regularly months later when cleaning it. I had no idea yet about the bugs and the mites and the dust baths involved in maintaining chickens, but I learned fast.

Before putting the coop together, though, we needed to create a foundation and make plans for a protective fence. And we couldn't cluck around. The chickens were growing and couldn't live in the house indefinitely. The little fluffballs were getting big and loud. We spent two weeks solidifying the plans, gathering the right tools and materials and supplies, and coordinating deliveries and a fairly large dump of gravel and sand for the foundational floor.

Tim was patient, and I was diligent. I was impressed by our ability to work as a team and maintain our consideration for each other. A sense of humor helped.

We also received help from our dear friends Alex Finch and his wife, Carrie. Carrie's sister had a place in the Catskills, and Alex, who grew up in Tim's theater company and was the youngest stage manager ever on Broadway, was the first assistant director on *For Life*. Shortly after the pandemic hit, they decided to get the hell out of New York City and they rented a house relatively near ours. The end of their two weeks of quarantine coincided with the start of construction on our coop, so they came over and entered our bubble.

Seeing friends in person after two months of isolation was wonderful and reenergizing for all of us. We didn't realize how starved we were for human contact until we were with them. As actors, we are highly emotional people, ready to laugh or cry on command, and just having someone ask, "How are you? How are your kids?" was almost overwhelming. Had we just come out of caves and realized other humans were roaming the earth with us? Not quite, but sort of. All of us had an eagerness to connect with other people.

They arrived around ten in the morning. Tim, the master of

the short order, made breakfast, and we sat outside and ate, talked (Do you have enough toilet paper? Have you found Clorox wipes? What have you been cooking? Did you watch Rachel Maddow last night?), and eventually got to work. Alex was adept with construction plans, and I had fun watching him and Tim go over the diagrams. The two of them were like Chip and Dale as they went back and forth over the dimensions for the posts that would hold up the chicken wire to keep out the predators. Alex was more mathematically inclined than my husband, but throw in the occasional drag off a joint the two of them shared and it was like they were trying to get NASA's Perseverance rover to Mars. They would have gone viral if we had put them on video.

Then we dug holes for the posts—or tried to; it was damn near impossible because the ground, as in most of the Catskills, was almost solid rock. No matter. We kept at it. Once the holes were completed, we laid the foundation: hardware cloth, sand, gravel, making it impenetrable from the ground up. Then we had the seven-hundred-pound coop delivered and set in the middle of what would become the run and added the fence, with the chicken wire, around and above it, then folded the excess hardware cloth up and around the whole thing, securing it with zip ties. After that the guys dug more post holes for the electric fence to keep the larger predators out, including bears. That was a crazy endeavor. Tim had to ram an eight-foot-long grounding rod into what was essentially a mountaintop. I don't know how he found the strength to do it, but he did it. The electric fence was wired up and we were in business.

The project took two weeks. When we finished, I had enough

bites and scrapes and cuts on my arms to make me look like a long-time tweaker. My hands were also ratchet and dry. I thought briefly about what it was like to get a manicure. It had only been a few months since my last one but it seemed like forever. I didn't care—and didn't really even want one. I had not just admiration for the Amish and every other craftsperson but also a new appreciation for those who built things, creating something where nothing existed before. My dad was like that; he had a workshop in the garage, and every time I smell sawdust, for a moment it reminds me of him. Sawdust and Clubman aftershave.

We showed the chickens their beautiful new home. Soon we would have fresh eggs, daily.

"Good job, everyone," Tim said.

My eyes lit up. That reminded me of a lovely and apropos line I once said as Laura on *Little House*:

"Every job is good if you do your best and work hard. A man stinks only to the ones that have nothing to do but smell."

A celebratory dinner capped the effort. I served leftovers and Advil. We reviewed the project, laughed at our mistakes, and marveled at our effort. I had helped dig postholes. I had learned to mix and pour concrete. I was covered in sunscreen, bug spray, sweat, and dirt. And I had also never been happier.

Life Begins the Day You Start a Garden

Where does hope come from?

Preachers, poets, and psychologists have tackled this question throughout human history. Pick your expert.

For me, it came from the view outside my window. It was the regenerative beauty of nature. It was spring, and it was gorgeous. And it was amazing to see. In the city, the warmth of the new season was greeted by throngs clad in T-shirts and flip-flops emerging from months in their apartments. In the country, it was marked by a symphony of life I had never before witnessed to this degree on a daily basis. Trees sprouted delicate little pastel-colored buds, white and pink and light blue. Butterflies and bees appeared. Hummingbirds showed up. Grass started to grow. At night, bats woke from their long sleep hungry for bugs.

Mother Nature announced the party was on.

And then, suddenly, BOOM, I woke up one morning, walked outside to greet the day—and the chickens—and I couldn't believe my eyes.

"Timmy! You've got to see this!"

He joined me outside.

"What?" he asked.

"Look," I said.

"At what?"

"Everything!"

I made a sweeping gesture across the yard that unspooled in front of us until it was met by a thick wall of trees. The forest floor was covered in ferns. There was grass everywhere. Flowers peeked up out of the ground all over the place. Over the next few days I spotted baby rabbits tentatively exploring their new world. Same with baby deer. They were everywhere, as if a bus had come by and dropped off a group. There were skunks, groundhogs, squirrels, porcupines, and raccoons. I felt like asking where everyone had been and how they had slept.

"It looks like we're not the only ones ready for spring," said Tim, taking off his work gloves after spreading bluegrass seed.

Recovered from the chicken coop, we were ready to tackle our next major project: planting a garden. We really were going through the motions of old-fashioned homesteaders. We found a place to live, fixed it up, waited out the winter, got our egg-laying chickens in order, and now we had to think about creating a garden where we could grow the food we would need to sustain ourselves. This turned out to be a much bigger project than the chicken coop. We had to determine where we wanted the garden; how to build it in order to protect it from all the critters who would see our efforts as a new Chick-fil-A in their neighborhood; what kind of soil we had; whether we had to build raised beds; how to rig up an irrigation system; and eventually what to plant.

But first things first. When Tim surfaced from his deep dive into the soil, he announced that we were going to have to build raised beds. There was so much rock beneath us—something we had discovered digging posts for the coop—that we would need a skip loader to overturn gigantic boulders and rip up underground rock if we wanted to plant a substantial enough garden. I was surprised.

"Did I know you can't just dig up the ground and plant a garden?" I asked rhetorically. "Apparently not."

"Yeah, because basically we're on a mountain," Tim said. "It may be flat now, but two hundred and fifty thousand years ago it was a mountain."

Still, it was extremely fertile. Pine, oak, and maple trees filled the woods. The floor beneath them was covered by ferns and grass. Flowers, as I knew from experience, took more work. The previous spring I had wanted to plant a butterfly garden of wildflowers and we had needed to rent a tiller to turn the soil. And that was just for a tiny flower garden in front of the house. The vegetable garden was an undertaking on a whole other scale.

Before we invested time, money, or effort, though, I reminded Tim of my unusual talent for killing just about anything green. Ice plants. Ivy. Even oleander—a plant that was supposed to kill me. Once I was put in charge, they shriveled up and died. The same was true with houseplants, orchids . . . basically anything with a stem and leaves. If you want your plants to die, let me babysit them. I just wanted to manage expectations.

"Don't worry, baby," he said, "the air here is so warm and thick with moisture from the lakes in the area, anything will grow."

We were standing in the yard in front of the house. I turned around, surveying potential sites for the garden, and shrugged.

"Okay, if you say so."

He wasn't really that interested in my cautionary anxieties. He had already communed with one of his YouTube boyfriends and committed to building the raised beds. This was after we had gone online to buy ready-made beds, which turned out to be stupid expensive compared to buying our own lumber. Even cheaper was cutting the lumber ourselves. To do that, though, we needed a table saw. Although that was costly, we figured we would use it later on and continue to save. So we ordered the table saw.

Once it was delivered, I put it together. In our home, I was queen of assembly. Anytime something came with instructions, I took the lead. I don't know why it is, but the clichés are true: Men won't ever ask for directions when they get lost and they don't have the patience to read the instructions before trying to assemble things. I say this as someone who is famous for having no sense of direction. I will walk out of the front door and turn the wrong way. But I will eventually ask for help. Tim had long ago turned the job of reading the instructions over to me, and we had reached the point where we agreed that he was not to take anything out of the box until I figured it out. Then I gladly turned to him and said, "Let's do this."

In fact, when it came time to tackle our composter, which arrived right after the table saw, Tim just left it to me and Carrie. She and Alex had returned to help build the garden. Alex and Tim waded back into crunching numbers for the poles and frames, and with neither of them going back to work anytime soon, they indulged in some pot before doing the math, while Carrie and I—I don't smoke pot—listened to their conversation.

Tim: It should be ten by ten by eight.

Alex: No, ten by ten by six.

Tim: Are you sure?

Alex: That's what I got.

Tim: Tell me again.

Alex: Tell you what?

Tim: Are you sure?

Alex: About what?

Tim: The measurements you got.

Alex: I can check.

Tim: Hang on a sec . . . Hon, what's for lunch?

None of it made any sense—except for lunch, of course—but Alex's math always checked out. Final plans called for flattening the area, digging postholes for the fencing, and putting down the hardware cloth, weed cloth, layers of mulch, gravel, and then sand. We were simultaneously preparing the soil for the beds and figuring out how to protect it from birds above, groundhogs below, and the bears, deer, bunnies, skunks, and squirrels coming from the outside.

From then on, it was two weeks of nonstop work. Deliveries of gravel, sand, and lumber arrived on time. The year before we had taken down a couple of trees that threatened to fall on the house and turned them into a giant mulch pile. The guys dug holes for the fence posts, straining as they worked around the boulders, cussing when, after hours of digging—it was more like fracking—they hit solid rock. Carrie and I cut the lumber and assembled the beds. At one point, Alex showed me how to change the torque on my drill to make it even stronger; then I leaned into it, driving in the screw and turning to the gang with a huge satisfied grin.

"Oh my God, this is amazing!" I shouted, sounding like I did as a twentysomething speeding up the Pacific Coast Highway in my then-boyfriend's Porsche.

After the beds were together, we found out the wood had been treated. We did some research and learned that you didn't want to use treated wood in a garden because the chemicals were un-healthy, but it was okay if they were lined with plastic. So Carrie and I climbed in with a staple gun—another fun tool—and fas-tened a layer of heavy plastic. Finally, everything came together. The beds were filled, and we added a sprinkler system, put up the deer-wire fence, then folded the hardware cloth over that, fastened it all with zip ties, cut and hung a door, and then, with several deer staring at us from a distance, their eyes laser beams of intense curi-osity, we were finished. I bent down and ran my fingers through the rich soil.

"Now, this feels sexy," I said.

The four of us stepped back and admired the work. Too tired to cook, we microwaved some food and poured cold drinks. Then we fell into lawn chairs and recapped the entire experience detail by detail. It was the postgame rehash of great plays, fumbles, and on-the-field heroics, and it was so necessary after spending the previous two weeks living in the moment, completely focused on whatever the job was at that second. We needed to look back and reward ourselves with a congratulatory, *Wow, we did that!*

"My arms are so tired I don't think I could scramble an egg," I said.

"Well, I cook the eggs," Tim said.

"How do your arms feel?" I asked.

"Are they still attached?" he said.

My hands were calloused and my fingernails were broken and full of dirt. They had never looked worse or felt more productive. I asked for a show of hands. Everyone's looked the same as mine.

"Ah, I see we all went to the same nail salon," I joked. "And got the same color—OPI's uber-trendy Soil Under the Nail."

Disgustingly dirty, sweaty, and sticky—and reveling in it—I described the numerous times Carrie and I had pushed the wheelbarrow to one of the piles of dirt and mulch, filled it up, then pushed it across the yard, dumped it in the raised beds, and went back for another load. It was like doing decades of exercise classes—Jane Fonda, Billy Blanks, SoulCycle, Peloton, and P90X—all in one. Each of us was sore from head to toe. We took turns describing our aches and pains, sounding as if we were in group therapy for day laborers.

Planting the seeds was almost anticlimactic. Carrie and I laid down corn, cucumbers, five types of tomatoes, various lettuces, green beans, watermelon, different-colored bell peppers, onions, peas, strawberries, and an array of herbs. I enjoyed thinking back on all the conversations Tim and I had had about what to plant and how it consumed us. Did you know peppers are considered fruit? Did you know corn kernels are seeds, and the silks coming out the top of the corncob are essential for pollinating the plants and are also considered to have medicinal benefits? There were so many intricacies and marvels inherent in these plants that we took for granted at the grocery store. I felt blessed to be learning so much. I also appreciated farmers more than ever.

Once the garden was completed, I feared we had probably planted too much too close together and as a result we might have a harvest of miniature veggies. We would have to wait and see. Live and learn, I said. At least the garden looked great, and fertile, a perfect place for seeds to germinate, grow, and turn into food—and the irrigation worked!

I imagined the garden full and green. In due time. For now, the beautiful earth would work its magic. I thought of the line from *The Little Prince*: "What is essential is invisible to the eye." Could it apply more to putting seeds in the ground and believing months from now they would grow tall and strong and teeming with fruits and vegetables?

Talk about faith.

But not in a religious sense. Tim and I felt an innate and undeniable sense of satisfaction from both the physical labor and our awareness that we were doing something to nurture ourselves and maybe pursuing something greater than ourselves. Down the line, I imagined giving our surplus eggs to the local food bank. I hoped for a harvest big enough to give fresh food to friends. We were also contributing to the planet, increasing our property value, and continuing to evolve and create this place that both of us had always thought we wanted to have but hadn't known how to do it.

Only we were doing it. We were learning. We were planning.

We were creating and fixing. We were boldly going where neither of us had gone before. We were working our asses off. And we were falling into bed shortly after dark for the most comforting deep sleeps of our adult lives. There is no better pillow than one filled with hopes and dreams.

Deer Me

"People . . . people who need people . . ."

The song Barbra Streisand made famous in her 1964 musical *Funny Girl* never had more meaning than it did nearly five months into the lockdown from the pandemic.

". . . are the luckiest people in the world."

Except for Alex and Carrie, we had not seen anybody. Tim did the grocery shopping, so he was able to have conversations with the folks who worked at the store, the checkers and stockers and baggers, all brave people deemed frontline, essential workers whom the rest of us suddenly saw in a new light as heroes.

Since I still wasn't venturing out, I was starved for contact—not just conversation. Real-life, face-to-face or mask-to-mask human contact. I watched *The Breakfast Club* one night just to feel like I was hanging out with friends.

One day a fan messaged me to say she had watched the *Little House* episode about a girl who sends notes down the creek in a bottle, asking for help. I was ready to plug a bottle with my own note. From my social media, I sensed many people felt the same way.

It was late May, and the weather was still mostly iffy punctuated by sporadic sunny days we could spend in T-shirts and flip-flops. I tended the garden, talked with the chicks, and kept up with friends and family via phone calls, email, and texts, though what I had to say might have been less scintillating than in the past. One day my best friend Sandy asked what was new. She understood the subtext when I responded, "Well, we learned that you can't run the griddle and the toaster and the coffeepot at the same time—not on the same wall."

At least I had my chickens. I spoke to them. I fed them. I let them out for walks in the midday sun. I made sure the heat panel in their coop was properly connected so they stayed warm during the nights that were below freezing. I complimented them on growing and said I was sure they would turn into beautiful women. I let them know that in their line of work, unlike Tim's and mine, laying an egg was considered a success.

I told them they were appreciated. I let them know they were seen and loved. In return they ran to me when I entered their area and they followed me around everywhere, especially when I had their favorite treats of iceberg lettuce or blueberries. Yet their affection was different from that of a cat or dog, no sloppy kisses or floppy snuggles.

It was just different. I had read that chickens responded to their caretakers, developed attachments, and learned their names.

A link to a January 2018 *National Geographic* had said, "Not only that, the birds can recognize and discern people based on their faces." I enjoyed all animal interactions. I had been that way my whole life. Once, while surfing in Hawaii, I was befriended by a dolphin. She sidled up to me while I was sitting on my board and circled nearby for the whole time I was in the water. It was like she made sure I was okay.

Another time, at a wild animal park in Tampa, Florida, a giraffe took a similar interest in me. We went out to feed the animals, and this one particular animal who was nearly fourteen feet tall and weighed around twenty-five hundred pounds wanted to be besties. She followed our truck and every time we stopped, she rested her head on my shoulder. I took it as a compliment.

Then there is my beloved French bulldog, Josephine. She was a freshly weaned twelve weeks old when I brought her into my life. My son Michael and I were going on tour with the *Little House* musical and I wanted to take a dog with us for companionship. I needed a small breed, and I'd had a fondness for French bulldogs ever since the early nineties, when I met my first one backstage at a talk show in New York City. Before Josephine, I actually got a Pomeranian whom we named Zoe. Sadly, she died of parvo two weeks later. I was absolutely devastated.

Then I found this fat, black brindle Frenchie. She looked like a piglet, or a bat or a monkey—no tail, smashed nose, pointy ears—and she was the funniest little creature I had ever seen. She spent four months at home with us in Tarzana before the tour started. Once we were on the road, she showed an innate if not unusual intelligence. She learned the ropes of airport security, quickly figured out the backstage area of each theater, and memorized the show so that she snoozed while I was onstage but was always waiting for me when I came back to change or take a break.

Despite the fact that she was extremely possessive and used to growl at Tim every time he walked into the room, she was extremely affectionate. She was like carrying around a blanket all day, though she was suffering the plagues of old age, blindness, and hearing loss. She slept most of the day. When I cleaned the chicken coop one day, though, she came outside and found me with her super-sensitive sniffer and hung out by my side until she had enough of the smell. Then she turned and went back inside the house.

Admittedly, she was spoiled. Think Eva Gabor on *Green Acres*. Tim and I may have gone country, but she was still a little bit Fifth Avenue. She slept in a pink cashmere sweater and wore a Louis Vuitton collar. Enough said, right?

One day I tried to make a new friend, a baby deer who emerged from the woods with the rest of her family—mother, brothers, sisters, cousins—as part of the great spring awakening. They came every day late in the morning to forage in the shrubs, clover, and flowers on our property. Watching them, first from the window and then from outdoors, I saw their eyes were wide and lips smacking with a delightful intention as they nibbled.

It was like they were at a restaurant after a long, hard winter of eating at home. I could relate.

This one particular young doe was more curious than the others. She started watching me as I watched her. I noticed the way she stood apart from the other deer, eyeing me with an interest that transcended the wariness that was so much a part of their nature. As with the dolphin, the giraffe, and my precious Josephine, I sensed we were connecting with each other. Every morning I opened the door, took a few steps outside, and stood as still as possible, seeking her out from the pack until we made eye contact. Then I offered a gentle hello.

I began to leave out little treats—an apple one day, watermelon the next, and so on. Each time I stood nearby, talking quietly to her ("Good morning, I left you another treat"), and each time, I noticed both of us tiptoed a little closer to each other, while the other deer watched from a safe distance, uninterested in making friends with a two-legged creature in overalls.

I don't know if this was right of me, if I was breaking an unwritten law, interrupting a natural order of things in the woods, but I wanted her to like me. In a way, I was back to being a kid on the set of *Little House on the Prairie*. Every time we had an animal on the show—a chimp, a wolf, a bear, an orangutan—I made a beeline for it. One time I carried around a little black panther all day.

"Are we friends yet?" Tim asked as he watched me with the deer.

"Working on it," I said.

"Are we having fun?"

"Muchly."

Clearly, I was trying to fill the hole created by the absence of friends and family, especially family. No need to call Dr. Freud, Dr. Oz, or Dr. Phil. I missed my children. And I really missed my grandchildren.

Then I got a surprise. My youngest son, Michael, formerly known as "the Thing in the Basement" but who was now a very handsome, talented twenty-five-year-old living with a roommate in Manhattan, wanted to visit. While holed up in New York City, he had envied all the industrious projects Tim and I had undertaken here in the country and ached to join us. Under normal circumstances, he could have come up and camped on the sofa. But with COVID, we'd had to tell him no, and it killed me.

This time, though, I asked him what day he wanted to come up. We finally had a way to be COVID safe—a ginormous RV. It was Tim's idea. We had planned and saved up to add another bathroom to our Cabbage, but COVID screwed up everything. That's when Tim pitched the idea of an RV. I had never imagined an RV as a source of life-changing excitement—to me, RVs had always been dressing rooms—but we were in a new world now, and after a bit of research, Tim and I found ourselves shopping for an RV in Port Jervis.

We arrived at the lot intent on looking at used RVs, but the salesman told us that new models were selling for the same price because of the slowdown due to COVID, and two minutes after he walked us through the interior, Tim and I were the owners of a brand-new house on wheels boasting a bedroom, a nook with bunk beds, one and a half baths, a full kitchen, and a sunken living room.

"A gas stove, too!" I gushed.

"It's perfect," Tim said.

We named it the Dressing Room; parked it on the side of the house, where it was not visible from the street; and took it upon ourselves to figure out the intricacies of all the hookups. Specifically we hooked up the sewer hose and created a downward slope so that it emptied straight into the cesspool under the outhouse. Then we connected the water and worked on the electricity. To complete the job, we needed our amazing electrician and pal, Dave Blethan, to create a separate box. Once that was finished, we called our local DirecTV installer to hook the RV up to the dish. The final touch was calling HughesNet to install a second Internet dish.

I let Josephine and the chickens wander over to the vehicle. "Well, guys, what do you think? Clearly something to cluck and crow about, right?"

It was. Tim and I offered to drive Michael back to the country. We had to go into the city anyway to pick up mail and water the one plant in our apartment, which turned out to be alive despite the neglect and abandonment. Our brief trip to the city was marked by the number of "permanently closed" signs that I saw on stores and restaurants. I thought of the movie *I Am Legend*, where the deer and lions are roaming through Times Square.

I was deliriously happy when Michael got into the car and I could see and hear him in person. But we didn't hug; per CDC guidelines, all of us were wearing masks and clear plastic face shields. We tried to keep a safe distance even in the car. Only a day or two before, he had participated in one of the many demonstrations that erupted in New York City and across the country to protest the death of George Floyd in Minneapolis, Minnesota, and we were nervous that he might have picked up COVID in the crowd.

But he assured us that he had worn a mask and washed his hands, so we relaxed a bit and we talked about the demonstration, and the gut-wrenching incident that had inspired it, all the way back to Highland Lake.

"It was a public lynching," Michael said.

"All I can think of are his kids and his mother," I said.

"His brothers, his family, his friends," Tim said. "The entire country watched it and felt it."

I certainly did.

"Before COVID, I was in my own lane," I said. "Like so many other people, I was just go, go, go, achieve, achieve, achieve. Make the money, pay the bills, go out to dinner, go to the movies, get my hair done, see my friends, do this, do that. Then George Floyd happened and it was *something*. I felt it. I saw the worst of society and wondered about my place in it. It woke me up, which I think is what being woke means. I realized I had to acknowledge some hard truths and get to work, and I hoped I wasn't alone."

"Right on, Mom," my son said.

Michael quarantined for two weeks in the Dressing Room. It was like a suite at the Four Seasons, room service, turndown service, and activities included. At night, I threw a red-and-white tablecloth over the picnic table and we enjoyed dinner outside under the stars. Michael brought an energy that crackled like lightning. Tim and I barraged him with questions about the George Floyd demonstration, and Michael obliged, walking us through his experience in the crowd in Union Square.

"It was extraordinary," he said. "People were wearing masks and being mindful. They were giving out water bottles and handing out food and hand sanitizer to each other. They were making sure people were all right. At the same time, they were doing what they needed to do to bring attention to something that we all found unacceptable."

"Was it mostly people your age?" I asked.

Michael shook his head. "A melting pot," he said. "Mostly young people, but all ages. All genders, all languages, all colors, and all of them there for a common purpose: to say that what happened is unacceptable."

I went inside and brought out refills of iced tea. The tranquil surroundings were a stark contrast to the violence we had witnessed on TV and the upheaval taking place in our cities. The woods were quiet save for the breeze rustling through the trees, the birds talking to each other, and the crickets chirping louder and louder. Josephine snoozed under my chair.

"Obviously I am aware of the privileged life I have lived," I said. "But now the obvious is painful. I am seeing myself in this privileged position to become outraged and upset by something that happened, but I don't have to deal with it every day, which itself is even more privilege. It's not my experience. It's not where I live. I'm not a Black woman, a Black mother raising Black children. So I don't have to deal with it. But . . ."

My throat tightened. All my emotions lodged there in a big lump.

"I'm thinking my complacency or my ignorance of what was going on, my blissful ignorance of what was going on all the time, may not have been helpful to other people, which is devasting right now."

Tim recalled the anti–Vietnam War demonstrations that were part of the cultural fabric and the generational divide when he was growing up in the late sixties and early seventies. We discussed the women's movement, the civil rights movement, and the systemic racism that continued to plague and divide America, which would soon be a country where people of color were in the majority.

"What about Breonna Taylor?!"

The twenty-six-year-old medical worker had been killed back in March during what the *New York Times* called "a botched raid" of her Louisville, Kentucky, apartment.

"How stupid are these police officers who busted into someone's house with a no-knock warrant and blew them away?" I said.

"Will charges be brought against those cops?" Michael asked.

Sadly, we knew the answer.

"Sickening," I said, adding that I had just seen a post on my Facebook feed where someone asked, "Why is it always a Black thing?" and I had responded, "Don't you mean why is it still a Black thing?"

"It's conditioning," Tim said. "A conditioning of ignorance."

"It's just not okay," Michael said.

We fell silent. I hated to think we had arrived at a dead end, but it felt like we had talked ourselves into a corner. My thoughts drifted. Throughout the pandemic, viewership of *Little House on the Prairie* had gone sky-high. People were finding the reruns on those networks that ran old shows, and they were watching with a new or perhaps renewed appreciation for the simple life and old-fashioned values we presented on the series. Episodes like "Plague" and "Quarantine" seemed timelier than when they aired in the mid-seventies.

But none touched a nerve like "The Wisdom of Solomon." In this 1977 episode, Todd Bridges guest-starred as the orphaned son of Mississippi sharecroppers who proposed exchanging his freedom for an education. When the episode re-aired, it set off a small firestorm on social media as viewers were once again shaken by hearing Todd Bridges ask Michael Landon, "Would you rather be

Black and live to be a hundred or white and live to be fifty?" and seeing Michael "Pa" Landon's reaction . . . which was speechless heartbreak.

Sadly, I and many others thought the question was still raw and loaded and disturbing nearly forty-five years after it first aired.

Where does change come from? I had flown to Washington, DC, the day after Donald Trump was inaugurated to take part in the Women's March. My friends and I were among the nearly half million women who showed up there—and more than three million across the country who protested peacefully and without incident. The crowd was massive and overwhelming and empowering. We were on the streets there for fifteen hours. I had never been more exhausted or exhilarated at the same time.

"We are mothers," Alicia Keys had told the marchers. "We are caregivers. We are artists. We are activists. We are entrepreneurs, doctors, leaders of industry and technology. Our potential is unlimited. We rise."

Earlier in the year, my seven-year-old granddaughter, Lulabelle, had attended a climate change rally with her mom in LA while carrying a sign that said I STAND WITH GRETA. She and her mom had also marched for Breonna Taylor and George Floyd. I hoped I had served as an example to them and that they in turn would do even more and better.

Listening to Michael, I sensed these kids were learning that change was something they couldn't leave for others. I believed they were going to do the work and all of us were going to be so much better for that. I am an optimist. I had hope.

But Tim had the final word. As the night grew late and our

impassioned conversation was punctuated by yawns, as I suspected was happening in households across the country, we tried to sum up in a way that would make sense and provide us with some comfort before bed. We didn't want to leave the last word to the crickets. Michael and I traded thoughts, and when we turned to Tim for his final thought, he grinned and delivered his memorable line from the movie *Field of Dreams*: "Do not sell this farm, Ray."

It was a simple message about not giving up on your dreams.

Do not sell this farm, Ray.

Indeed.

The Bear Necessities

"Look," Michael said about a week into his quarantine. "Deer."
It was late morning, and until then, my son had been sleeping late, as those his age tend to do, and missing these visits from our four-legged neighbors. If we hadn't seen Michael by ten or later, Tim, who usually got up a little before six, would ask if he was still incubating in the RV, and I would say, "Please, God, not incubating anything."

But gradually Michael rose earlier and earlier and got into the rhythm of country life. What he found is the sheer delight of morning: the crisp air, the music of the chirping birds, the waking critters, and the clean slate of the day ahead. With the sun shining, it felt like a cup of possibilities was being served.

And it was. Actually, before Michael woke up that day, I called Tim out to the garden, where I showed him several baby cucumbers and a bunch of new yellow flowers on our tomato plants. We were going to be inundated with tomatoes! We were also getting close to having ripe strawberries. Once Michael joined us, I showed him the garden. I also showed him the pesky Japanese beetles I spotted and how I zapped them with a home-brewed formula of rubbing alcohol, vegetable oil, and dish soap.

"Gotta do that about every ten days," I said.

Michael was not interested. He was mesmerized by the deer munching their breakfast only a few yards away. I could see that he was trying to figure out why they were undeterred by our proximity.

"They're used to us," I said. "Let me introduce you to my friend."

Pointing out the young deer whose trust and friendship I had been nurturing, I showed Michael the way I set food out and drew the deer close to me. She came within six feet before rejoining her bunch—the brunch bunch. I was making friends, I explained. Michael was impressed.

Over the next week or so, I also introduced the way we free-ranged the chickens later in the day, letting them roam around the yard, eating and pecking whatever and wherever they wanted. I explained that some people leave their chickens out all day, occasionally losing one to a hawk or an eagle or a raccoon.

"But I'm a little crazier about our chickens," I said.

"Obviously." He smiled.

I may have spoiled them. When the temperature soared into the eighties one day, I filled their water bowls with frozen blueberries and cucumbers. I had noticed them panting and wanted to know how to prevent them from overheating. The research I did said to give them more fruits and vegetables, which contain water, rather than grain and corn, which are dehydrating. I thought, Of course, I'll make them spa water. In the late afternoon, while they free-ranged, Tim played the guitar for them, which they also seemed to enjoy. At sundown, they made their way back to their coop. They were going home to roost. It was instinctive. Several times I forgot to unlock the gate to their run and they stood outside, mad as cluck, waiting for me to open it.

"I love the ritual of being outside with them and watching their silly personalities. It's the best show on television," I said.

"They're almost four months old," Tim mused. "I wonder what older chicks will be like."

"They'll be like me," I cracked.

But enough talk about chickens. Tim came home one day from a trip to the nearby town of Narrowsburg practically bursting with excitement. He had seen a mother bear and her two cubs walking along the road not too far from our house. I'd had no shortage of animal sightings of my own, including an enormous eagle eating something it found on the side of the road. I had also seen eagles fly overheard. They were impressive creatures. But I had never seen a bear—and I wanted to so badly.

"I can't believe you weren't in the car with me," Tim said.

For the next two weeks, I looked for bears every time we got in the car. I craned my neck far to the right and then far to the left, which wasn't easy because I was experiencing some neurologic pain in my spine. But I would have turned my head all the way around like Linda Blair in *The Exorcist* if it had been possible. That's how badly I wanted to see a bear. Then one day the bear found me. I didn't even have to look for him.

We were between breakfast and lunch. Tim was building a new trellis from PVC pipe in the garden, and Michael and I were putting together a circular saw that Tim had ordered. The parts were spread out on the lawn under one of our big pine trees. Josephine was lying close by. The sprinklers were on. We were also streaming music loud.

I noticed Josephine sit up suddenly. At her age, she rarely did anything that fast. When I turned toward her, I saw her ears had perked up and her nose pointed toward the garden. She was staring at something. Then I looked and saw what appeared to be the back end of one of those large poodles, a black standard poodle. I thought, Oh God, whose dog got out? Then I reconsidered that assessment. Who had a poodle up here? No one. This was golden retriever country. My French bulldog was the only city dog in the vicinity.

When the giant poodle lifted its head, I had a clear view of its profile and saw it was quite unmistakably and magnificently a bear. The bear was about the size of a large German shepherd. So it was not a fully grown bear. It was not a baby, either. My heart raced; my blood pressure skyrocketed; my nervous system went on red alert.

"Timmy!" I yelled. "Tim! Tim!"

Tim didn't hear me above the music and the sprinkler the first half a dozen times I shouted his name. Then he looked up.

"What, babe?"

"Bear!"

Josephine started to move toward the bear, as if she wanted to play. I grabbed her and shouted something to Tim, who shook his head, not understanding, because whatever I was saying came out as a slur of gibberish. My sudden fear confounded me, because I had worked with bears on the set of *Little House*. More specifically,

I had worked with the bear who had played Gentle Ben on the television series *Gentle Ben*. He was the least frightening bear ever. He was trained to work for Tootsie Rolls.

The bear in our yard, of course, was not trained at all.

Once it was established that we had noticed each other, the bear began walking toward us. I could see him sniffing, as if he were trying to determine whether Tim, Michael, and I were giant Tootsie Rolls. Completely unafraid, he was casual and curious, not menacing. He looked like he wanted to ask if we had any food. Or if we might be food ourselves.

"Michael, let's get inside," I said. "Move slowly—but fast."

Tim was already backing toward the house. The bear continued to move toward us, wondering where we all were going and why. He stopped by the garden, distracted by something. Perhaps the smell of our strawberries. By this time, we were watching him from inside the house. We were safe. But my mind flashed on the chickens. Were they safe?

"Destruction could happen out there," I said to Tim and Michael.

It didn't. The bear lost interest and wandered out of view. I used this reprieve to call Fawn Schneider, my friend from animal control who had helped get the squirrels out of our walls. I left a message on her cell. She called back twenty minutes later. After listening to my description of the encounter, she had questions.

"Not afraid, right?" she asked.

"No, he was curious," I said.

"Although I'd have to see, it sounds like about a yearling," she said. "Sometimes they get separated from their mama bears in the winter. They get rescued and rehabbed and they lose their fear of humans. He could be one of those guys."

"We want to be neighborly, but we don't want to socialize," I said. "What do we do?"

"They don't like loud noises," she said.

"Roger that," I said.

So Tim and Michael and I formed the Highland Lake Cookware and Cast Iron Scaredy Cats Band. We grabbed pots, pans, and mixing spoons from the kitchen and ventured outside banging and clanging and scanning the area for the bear. We spotted the bear on the other side of the garden and shed, about one hundred yards away. He saw us, too, and took a few steps in our direction, at which point we banged and clanged ever more vigorously, and louder, which worked. He turned around and disappeared into the woods.

"Well, I'm shaking like a leaf! That was scary . . . and, honestly, a little fun and exciting, too," I said.

For the next few days, I kept a wary eye out for him. But we had no sightings. I figured we were not going to see him again. A few weeks later, I was in the house and heard Tim outside shout, "Bear!" It was like an alarm went off at a fire station. I jumped up, grabbed a pot and a wooden spoon, and sprinted outside making as much noise as I could. I beat the pot so hard that I broke the wooden spoon and sent half of it flying across the yard.

But it seemed to work. The bear turned and sauntered away from the house. Then he thought better of it and reversed course back toward us. The two of us, me and the bear, made eye contact. He was like, Hey, you're good but you broke your spoon. Still, he wasn't threatening. He seemed amused.

Tim wasn't. When he saw the bear moving toward me, Tim, a former semipro baseball starting pitcher who had played in a championship-winning over-forty league through the previous summer, picked up a rock, took aim, and hurled it at the bear. He nailed the bear squarely in the shoulder. I heard the thwack from where I stood across the yard. The bear did not wait around to see if Tim could throw another strike. He quickly vanished from sight.

One afternoon about a week later, I looked out the window and spotted the bear again. This time he was sniffing under the unplugged electric fence surrounding the chickens. I yelled, "Bear," and Tim and I ran outside with our noisemakers. Only we didn't see the bear. We looked right and left and front and back without seeing him. Then we looked up—and there he was! In the tree above the chicken coop, looking down at us, wiggling his nose, and seeming cool and content, like he got a good seat for the matinee.

We did the usual with our pots and pans and he took off. Back inside, I googled "how do you keep bears away from your chickens?" I half expected Google to return with, "I don't know. How do you do it?" But we got an answer: air horns. So we ordered a bunch of air horns and put them near every door and window in the house and the RV. They worked. The next time we saw the bear, we gave him the air horn treatment and he ran off.

But I learned that air horns had their limits. One day I was at the house by myself. Tim was in the city, at a virtual read-through for his ABC series *For Life*. I walked out to the shed to get some tool and saw the bear. He was maybe fifty yards to my right, in front of the house, and he had his nose buried in the ground. Sniffing, snorting, and shaking, he could not have been more oblivious to me. I blasted the air horn, to no effect. He didn't move.

I tiptoed a little closer and blew the air horn again. He kept his nose to the ground. I inched even closer and saw what was riveting his attention—his head was buried in a cloud of bees. I realized there must be an underground hive full of honey. Good for him but not for me. I was scared of the bear and deathly allergic to bees. I wanted nothing to do with any of them. If I got attacked or stung, I was a goner.

I wanted to get the hell out of there. As I hurried back into the house, something stung me. I felt the pinch on my ribs, just beneath my heart and above my abdomen. It must have flown up my dress. I ran into the house and called Tim, who didn't answer. He was in his read-through. I texted him and got a call back moments later.

"I got stung," I said anxiously. "Do I call nine-one-one? What do I do?"

Tim's voice was calm. "How are you feeling right now?"

I took a breath and did a quick inventory of my vitals, expecting to feel my heart racing and my throat swelling, along with other weirdness. But I didn't feel any of that.

"I'm . . . I'm okay, I think," I said.

"Really?"

"I can breathe."

"Take the Benadryl just to be on the safe side," Tim said.

"Hold on," I said, putting down the phone while I got a glass of water and found the blister pack of antihistamine. "Okay, I'm back," I said.

"Did you take one?" Tim asked.

"I took three," I said. "Just to be really safe."

When no adverse effects occurred after twenty minutes, I deleted 911 from my phone and called the exterminator instead. Mine had to have been the most high-pitched, hysterical voice they had heard in ages.

"I need you guys here right now," I said. "I can't go outside. There was a bear in my front yard. There's a beehive underground. It's got to go."

"Sorry," the woman on the other end said, "but we're completely booked."

"You don't understand," I said. "I'm home alone. My husband is in the city. I've been stung once and I haven't reacted so far, but I am really, really, really allergic. And if I get stung again, I'm in big trouble."

"Okay, ma'am, we'll send someone out," she said.

I was still managing to keep myself together—actually, I was kind of buzzing from the Benadryl. The bear took off, shaking off the swarm of bees, about fifteen minutes before the exterminator arrived. He got out his equipment, slipped on his protective beekeeping gear, and smoked the hell out of those nasty invaders. About twenty minutes later, he knocked on the door, finished.

"Stupid bear," he said. "There was no honey. They were yellow jackets, not bees." Before I could heave a really huge sigh of relief, the three Benadryls hit me like a hammer, so I spent the rest of the day on the recliner watching chick flicks and eating mac 'n' cheese.

Even though the bear had scared us quite a bit, we still loved that he was a part of the wilderness we lived in. Sadly, that was our last encounter with the bear. Days and weeks passed without a sighting. Our level of concern dropped from high alert and constant lookout, to not even thinking about whether a bear was in our midst, to even missing the big guy. I even felt a twinge of guilt for the way we had treated him. Had we been too harsh and aggressive in our noisemaking? Were we not welcoming enough? Did our property fail him in some way? Were we missing bees and hives and the sweetness of the honey they produced?

Why couldn't we all somehow live as one? Weren't we supposed to? Or was I mistaken in thinking that was part of the goal?

Those were really the questions. What was our role in this busy and full ecosystem that Tim and I had made ourselves part of? This was our property, but did that extend to our furry and feathery neighbors? How much belonged to them? Did we have a responsibility to them? In order for our garden and surrounding plant and tree life to survive, and thrive, we not only needed to respect the complexity of nature, we also had to embrace and nurture it. What was good for the soil, the vegetation, the wildlife that also called it home?

When you live in nature, are you supposed to live among it? Or are we humans entitled to bend it to our will? If so, how much?

I knew we had to celebrate the diversity of our neighbors—and our neighborhood. Were we succeeding?

Of course, these questions weren't confined to our little Cabbage in the country. They were some of the questions that defined our time as we addressed issues like climate change and how we got along with each other. Then one day in the early fall, Tim came back from visiting with our neighbor who owned the land beyond our chicken coop, something like twenty acres with a tiny hunting shack. He had it up for sale. Tim had a glum expression as he walked into the kitchen and took off his hat. He sighed.

"What, babe?" I asked.

"Our neighbor said he was up here last week with a friend, and his friend shot a bear."

I felt a clutch in my chest.

"Our bear?" I asked.

Tim started to say something but stopped. He shrugged sadly instead.

I glanced over at the air horn by the window, got up, and walked over to the kitchen door. I looked outside. The chickens were pecking the ground and clucking in their coop. The garden was growing. A soft breeze ruffled the leaves in the trees. Overhead, wisps of white clouds drifted past. Through my sadness for our bear, I could see nature was our greatest teacher, and even when we were unable to understand the lessons, we could still feel them.

Part Three

And we've got to get ourselves
Back to the garden.
JONI MITCHELL

Summertime, and the Living Is Covered with Sunscreen and OFF!

Summer swept in a couple weeks early, and it was divine. I was ready for the warm weather. It was mid-June, and within days of each other, we celebrated Tim's birthday and picked our first strawberries of the year, which gave me a deeper understanding of what John Lennon meant when he said, "Strawberry Fields forever."

My goodness, I have to say that first strawberry was sublime, a supersweet candy with the perfect combination of soft and crisp that flooded my mouth with flavor. I savored the strong, sweet, refreshing taste and chewed very slowly, hoping it wouldn't end. Where was Tim? I looked around until I found him and then purred, "Oh. My. God."

I said the same thing the day I picked my first green beans off the vine. While tending to the garden one morning, I noticed a few beans that looked ripe. The others were only just moving into the pod stage from their initial bloom as flowers, but these early arrivals called out to me. There was no other reason for me to notice them. They wanted to be eaten, to show off, to let me know this was more than the strawberry show.

A quick twist, and they were off the vine and in my hand. I used the water bottle I'd stuck in the pocket of my dress to rinse them and popped one in my mouth. The crunch was sharp and loud, and it released a sweetness that I never would have associated with green beans. Wow, that was amazing.

"Timmy!" I shouted.

I didn't know where he was, but my husband heard me call his name and appeared in the garden.

"You have to taste one of these," I said, offering him the beans. "I just picked them."

He tried one.

"Delicious," he said.

"I know," I said. "I've never eaten one straight off the vine. I'm thinking I might have to dispense with the sauté pan and just bring the dinner table and chairs out to the garden."

"Sure," he said. "Just throw some salt at the plants—"

"And some melted butter," I interjected.

"And we can graze," he said.

It being summer, I was more than happy to support such ideas. One day our friends Alex and Carrie showed us a secret cove on a lake about fifteen minutes from our place. Michael, though about to go back to the city, joined us on the outing. It was sublime. The sun pushed the temperatures into the eighties. Alex built a shade sail, tying a large sheet to a tree and anchoring the ends with sticks and rocks, and we settled in for the day. I didn't think summer could be any more relaxing. The water was clear. Eagles from a nearby sanctuary soared overhead. Occasionally a fish broke the surface. Birds sang to each other. We swam, fished, played Frisbee, and enjoyed the tranquility of being by ourselves.

Michael shouted from the water, "Look, Mom, no mask!"

We laughed.

"I almost forgot that we're in the midst of a pandemic," I said.

"Let yourself forget it," Tim said.

"It almost feels like normal," I said.

It was as if our 100 SPF sunscreen blocked out more than harmful ultraviolet rays.

Alex raised his beer. "Here's to normal."

"Is anybody hungry?" I asked.

Everyone raised their hand and followed it with a happy chorus of *me-me-me*s. I opened up the picnic basket I had packed and took out the most savory and satisfying thing one can possibly eat when picnicking on the beach: Cold. Fried. Chicken. (Let those three words rest on your taste buds for a few seconds.)

As far as I'm concerned, cold fried chicken is a quintessential summer dish. You don't want it in the winter, although I will eat cold fried chicken at the drop of a hat any time of the year. When I make fried chicken, I always make a few extra pieces to ensure I have some leftovers to nosh on the next day. Regardless, I know some people might not have ever tasted cold fried chicken. I also know other people may not be a fan. Perhaps you fall into one of those categories. If you are a vegetarian or vegan, I understand. If not and you've never tasted it, my heart aches for you. You have missed out.

Fried Chicken
(Cold or Hot—You Decide)

2 cups all-purpose flour
5 tablespoons Old Bay
  seasoning
2 tablespoons salt
1 tablespoon fresh ground
  pepper

2 (4- to 5-pound) fryer
  chickens, cut into
  pieces, rinsed, and
  patted dry
Vegetable oil, for frying

Mix the flour, Old Bay, salt, and pepper in a large zip-top plastic or brown paper bag. Drop in the chicken pieces and shake to coat; you will probably have to do this in batches.

Pour the oil into a 12-inch deep cast-iron skillet to a depth of 1 inch. Heat it over high heat until a drop of water bubbles when it hits the oil. Shake any excess seasoning mix off the chicken pieces and put them skin side down in the pan, working in batches if necessary to avoid overcrowding. Cover and cook for 15 minutes, then remove the cover, turn the chicken, and cook, uncovered, for another 15 minutes, or until golden brown. (Watch closely that it doesn't burn; you might need to reduce the heat to medium-high.) Drain and dry the chicken on paper towels.

For cold fried chicken, let the chicken reach room temperature, then wrap in foil or place in a zip-top plastic bag and put in the fridge.

Fresh, hot fried chicken is itself wonderful, but something magical and downright miraculous happens when it is left overnight in the fridge to chill. The crispy crust stays crunchy, while the fat beneath the skin congeals and becomes chewier, and the flavor in the meat seems to intensify in the mouth like a time-release treat.

If you still don't get it, think cold pizza. Cold fried chicken is kind of the same thing but not really.

We devoured every piece that I had packed, as well as a big old tub of coleslaw and giant chunks of watermelon and some vegetarian delights for Carrie. Was the meal gourmet? Who cared! This was the age of COVID and no one had their fancy pants on anymore. I had heard—anecdotally, of course—that many people had given up on pants altogether.

This simple life—or #prairielife, as I called it—agreed with me. As busy as I always seem to be, I think I am an inherently still person. I am happiest reading or knitting, with Josephine snoring at my feet. But I have never had the time to be still. I spent so much of my life going and doing and being seen at the right places; signing up for the best workouts; wearing the trendiest clothes; running and schlepping and coaching and carpooling and working. And working. Always working. Starting when I was cast on *Little House on the Prairie* at nine years old. I was ten when it premiered.

But with our biggest household projects finished, Tim and I, having completed our daily chores, usually turned to each other around midafternoon and asked, "What's next on the agenda? What do you want to do?" We found ourselves with something we hadn't had since childhood—free time.

Want to go for a walk?

Read?

We could write a movie.

Or watch one.

Or play Jenga.

We did all of the above. Our kids were grown up and our industry was shut down. We were still. As dire as COVID, climate change, hatred, and politics had made life in the US, I realized that I could control only what I could control, which wasn't much beyond our immediate surroundings, and as a result, I granted myself permission to be still.

I recalled an Italian phrase I'd learned from the book *Eat, Pray, Love*—*dolce far niente*. It means the beauty of doing nothing, the pleasure of relaxed idleness. I thought of the ways society could benefit physically, mentally, and psychologically if we made relaxed idleness a priority. What would be the harm in making time in the day for yoga, walking outdoors, reading, or meditation—something other than the nonstop, do-or-die compulsion to work that seemed to consume and stress people out.

Do you live to work? Or do you work to live?

Here in the country, the answer was obvious. I watered and weeded the garden every day. If I didn't, nothing would grow.

The fruits of such labor, or rather the vegetables of such labor, were suddenly visible. Our miracle garden—called such because it was a miracle that I had not killed these plants—produced its first harvest on July 5, a Sunday that Tim and I will forever remember as the day I brought a basket of basil, sage, cilantro, and lettuce into the kitchen.

"Looky," I said, beaming with pride.

"It's beautiful," Tim said. "It's art."

"It's dinner!"

I arranged the fresh greenery on my kitchen counter, snapped a picture, and posted it on my Instagram page. The reaction was instantaneous. "Aren't fresh herbs and veggies the best!" one woman commented. Another said she had just planted herbs in her own backyard, adding, "You have the same paper towel holder that I have."

By this time, we'd had our chickens almost four months, about the length of time needed to tell with assurance whether our chicks were hens or roosters. If you are among those whose primary encounters with poultry take place in grocery stores, drive-thrus, and diners, you might be curious to know that cockerels—aka little boy chickens—develop pointy feathers around their neck and tail, while the feathers on a hen—the girls—are rounder. A rooster will also often have a brighter-colored comb and wattle.

When we inspected our original Deathlayer brood, we found that only two of our seven chicks, Henny and Penny, were egg-laying girls. The others were all dudes. Before those boys started to fight among themselves—and they were starting to cock-a-doodle-doo quite a bit—we arranged with the guy who sold them to us to trade them in for two pullets, slightly older female chickens that Timmy named Cotton and Coco; three sexed baby chicks, who were immediately referred to as the Andrews Sisters; and a fourth little one we named Peep.

The pullets stayed in the coop with Dr. Fauci, Henny, and Penny. We housed the young'uns in the kitchen. They were as tiny as the newborns we'd had before, little beaked babies with down-like feathers, and adorable. As soon as I had some free time the next day, I scooped Peep up, plopped myself on the recliner, and had a little welcome-to-the-family tête-à-peep with her that went like this:

"Yes?"

"Peep, peep, peep."

"Well, of course."

"Peep, peep, peep."

"Whatever you say."

"Peep, peep, peep."

"Absolutely. I totally understand."

A day or two later, I cornered Tim in the living room and told him to get ready for a thrill. I slipped into the kitchen and returned with all four babies—"The Littles," I announced. I set them on Tim's chest. One of the Andrews Sisters inched herself under his chin and another one of the sisters sidled right up against his whiskered cheek. The girls peeped and chirped. They presented an adorable picture of a man and his birds.

Eat your heart out, George Clooney and Brad Pitt, I thought. Timothy Busfield is a chick magnet!

We laughed every day. I had no idea how life could feel so charmed on a budget in the middle of a pandemic in a country struggling under a corpulent despot who served McDonald's at the White House, suggested fighting COVID by ingesting Clorox wipes (or something close to that ridiculousness), and repeatedly declared himself "your favorite president." Obviously, he wasn't my favorite. I read the news every morning but stayed away from watching cable news throughout the day. I checked the Johns Hopkins COVID global map. I looked at the New York State map, which enabled me to click on my county and find out how many tests, cases, hospitalizations, and deaths had been recorded in our area. Before dinner, I allowed myself another dose of headlines. I asked what the hell was going on, and then I tried to read well-researched and sourced articles that gave me answers.

I tried to know enough—not more, not less. That was my way of exerting control over a situation that had turned the world upside down. With knowledge, I was able to find some inner calm. Being informed let me sit on the beach and fall asleep more easily, though that didn't happen as often as I'd like to think. I have a sense that just the memory of a good nap has its own rejuvenating appeal.

Walks and hikes were part of the daily routine. Tim marked the delayed start of the Major League Baseball season—probably his favorite of all the seasons—by ordering several dozen Wiffle balls and a couple of bats from Amazon and organizing home run derbies. We played across from the Cabbage. A line drive off the house was a hit. Launching the ball onto the roof was a home run. Over the roof was a grand slam.

I lost track of how many times we played over the summer, but none of the games were as memorable as the first one.

"Hey, honey, want to hit first?" he asked, standing in the middle of the yard next to two buckets of balls. "I'll throw it underhanded."

After a couple of practice swings and a few misses, I hit the ball onto the roof. I hit a few more, too.

"Baby, why don't you try a couple left-handed?" Tim said.

"Really?" I said.

I stepped over the rock doubling as home plate, altered my stance, and smacked the next four onto or over the roof. I thought I was ready for the pros. Then we took our Wiffle balls with us when we went to Alex and Carrie's for dinner. Carrie, a star softball player in high school, kicked our asses.

Another night we set up an inflatable movie screen in our backyard, sat in folding chairs, and ate buttered popcorn. As much as I already knew the power of movies to transport an audience, I think the four of us experienced a whole new thrill by watching *Alien* under a sky full of stars and with an assortment of critters spying on us from the woods. I know that I did. It only heightened the tension I felt when Tom Skerritt was about to get brutally murdered and Sigourney Weaver warned, "Oh God! It's moving right toward you! Move! Get out of there! Behind you! Move!"

We were biding time until more of the vegetables and fruits in our garden were ready to be harvested. My work in the garden the past week or so had been an exercise in self-restraint. I so badly wanted to pick everything but knew they weren't quite ready, especially the green beans, which seemed to glisten like gorgeous sunbathers lying around a pool in Miami. No, no, no, I told myself, slow down, woman, it's too soon.

Finally, the day came when the cucumbers signaled their readiness to be lovingly and gratefully brought into the house. I dressed appropriately for this Oscar-level occasion, walking the grass and dirt carpet to the garden in tie-dye T-shirt, comfy bib overalls, Crocs with strawberries on them, a wide-brimmed hat, and my hair in braids. I easily imagined Giuliana Rancic describing me as looking vintage hippie circa 1975 and asking the usual red-carpet questions.

Who dressed you today?

Well, I did. I got into my clothes all on my own.

And your shoes?

Crocs—strawberry ones.

Well, you look marvelous. Enjoy yourself.

I had planted a mix of English and Boston pickling cucumbers, the latter especially for making sour pickles. They were short and firm, their skin much thinner than their longer, more traditional English cousins. I brought in a ton of them. They arrived on the plant in an exciting plentitude that had me imagining all the different types of pickles we could make—whole, bread and butter, etc. I wasn't doing any dills. For those, people recommend Kirby cucumbers, and I hadn't planted any of those.

Anyway, I scrolled through pickling recipes on the Internet until I found the ones that appealed to me. I had made jellies and jams before, so I had the canning equipment already available. Everything else was simple. For the sour pickles, I made a brine with water, salt, garlic, chili peppers, and dill among the major ingredients, brought it to a boil, sliced the cucumbers and put them in jars, poured the brine over them, closed the jar, boiled the jar, and put them in the pantry to sit and ferment for at least three days.

The bread and butter pickles took virtually the same steps, only with a set of different ingredients, including thinly sliced onions, apple cider vinegar and white vinegar, both brown and white sugar, and mustard and celery seeds. When they were in the jars, I put those into the fridge to chill for a few days.

Three days later, with Tim watching, I tried one of the bread and butter pickles. My face said everything. I didn't have to utter a single word to express the fireworks going on in my mouth, but I did anyway: "These. Are. Stupid." I alternated between the two types but brought jars of pickles to every meal and every outing to the beach. Later, after Michael left, Tim's son Willy, his girlfriend (now-wife) Angella, and two of her three sons visited, and they cleaned us out of pickles after a day. They described them the same way as I did—stupid.

Besides pickles, we had green beans, more varieties of lettuce, and several types of tomatoes, which ripened weekly in thrilling abundance. Walking into the house with a full basket of produce that came from my yard filled me with joy. Our first salad with lettuce, tomatoes, cucumbers, peppers, and herbs from the garden, with just a little sprinkle of oil and vinegar, was unlike any salad we had ever eaten. The word *stupid*, clearly overused in our tiny household, came up again and again. *The salad tonight is stupid!* Nothing beat running out to the garden and grabbing some lettuce, a pepper, and a couple of tomatoes; slicing them up; tossing them together; portioning it all out; and watching our eyes light up. We grew that! *It's stupid good! It's so good it's stupid!*

Back when I had planted the seeds, I had read somewhere—probably the Internet—that farming required good soil, hearty seeds, enough water, hard work, and above all else, tons of faith. Now, months later, this bounty on our table was the fruit of that faith—a harvest that was proof of small miracles. I am not a religious person, and we didn't say grace, but I still sensed an amen was appropriate.

What Brings You to This Nape of the Neck . . . Um . . . Neck of the Woods?

"Listen." Tim and I paused in the yard and considered what we heard (a light breeze rustling leaves, a squawking bird, a squirrel hopping to a higher tree branch) and everything we didn't hear (the roar of cars and motorcycles, the clang of trucks bouncing over potholes, emergency sirens, and all the other noise we used to hear in the city). It was quiet. And lovely. And peaceful. And something to appreciate.

I found the sound of nothing to be quite soothing. The chickens and rooster occasionally sounded off, and every so often we heard the rumble of a passing car or pickup truck, but generally there was quiet. As I grew more attentive to the lack of noise, though, I heard so much more—the buzzing of cicadas and crickets, beetles and bees, yellow jackets and fireflies, dragonflies, frogs and grasshoppers; the howls and screams of coyotes, eagles, hawks, owls, warblers, and peewees; and the knocking of woodpeckers. I also heard myself breathe and think and relax.

This glorious silence was a preferable alternative to the ugly and unladylike groans that came out of me in response to the severe pain in my fifty-six-year-old neck. I mostly expressed the discomfort by whimpering, "*Ow-ow-ow!*" But if I turned wrong, tweaked a nerve, and the pain was really bad, I let out a profanity-laced yelp that let everyone in the vicinity know I was hurting. "Ow, fuckity, OW!!!"

The condition was not pretty or new. Back in January, I had started suffering pretty serious pain in my neck (AGAIN!) and a host of referred problems down my shoulder all the way to the numb and tingling fingers of my right hand. Knowing where that was going to lead, I saw a surgeon in New York, who determined that a spinal fusion I'd had done four years ago—my second cervical spinal procedure—had failed, and diagnosed some stenosis and other problems in my previously repaired spine. Though he recommended that I not do anything immediately, he said that if I did choose to have surgery, he would go in through the back of my neck and blah-blah-blah.

That caused my red flags to shoot straight up to full mast. Based on my experience, I knew that if you're going to have surgery on your neck, unless it's an absolute emergency, like you have broken your neck in an accident, you never go in through the back because of how much longer it takes to heal the tendons, ligaments, and muscles. As a result, I sent my MRI images, X-rays, and a hand-drawn sad face to Dr. Bray, who had done my very first fusion in 2003 and had repaired my broken back in 2010.

The Newport Beach, California–based doctor found the fusion he had done was fine but the one done in Michigan in 2016 had never fused; it was a rare complete fail, so much so that the plastic hardware the surgeon in Michigan had put in there had broken loose and was boring holes in my vertebrae. He also saw bone spurs and compression. He felt that I had a six-month window during which he could, hopefully, take all of that hardware out and give me an artificial disc. Eager to address the problem, I began gearing up for a possible trip to Newport Beach and the surgical procedure in March. Then COVID hit and all nonemergency procedures were canceled.

Finally, in July, I heard he was back doing surgery on a non-emergency basis, and at the end of the month, we had a telemedicine check-in. By this time, I was experiencing agonizing pain but also increased numbness and tingling in my fingers. Dr. Bray advised having the surgery as soon as possible, which I would have done. But getting preapproved by insurance turned into a long, frustrating rigmarole because everyone at the insurance company was working from home and they were seriously backlogged. My wait would last until November—as would the taxing inconvenience of my longtime companion, chronic pain.

Although I had my first neck injury in the late nineties and have spent decades living with and managing pain—sometimes successfully, other times unsuccessfully—I try not to dwell on this aspect of my life. Everyone lives with something, be it physical, mental, or both. These recurring spinal injuries and subsequent issues are what I bear. Fortunately, I have a high tolerance for my own pain, but it has also taught me to have an intolerance for not understanding and doing nothing about the pain others suffer.

How could anyone feel otherwise?

It bothered me that so many appeared to be that way. Parts of the US were dealing with an opioid epidemic. Children were going hungry. Racism had burst out into the open. The president faced impeachment. Politicians fed their own desire for power, creating more problems than they solved. The Rust Belt despaired as they fell further behind an increasing technologically driven economy. America appeared to be breaking down into warring factions. Institutions were attacked; alternative facts and conspiracy theorists were embraced. Then there was the existential reality of climate change dooming human life. And this was all before we were hit by COVID and began each day with a new death count.

The country was in pain. We were grieving. We were headed for some major PTSD. And not only was our dear leadership not talking about this, but they were also causing it or denying it or spreading misinformation or all of the above. A few months later, columnist Peggy Noonan would write, "It seems a funny thing to say of public policy, but so much of what doesn't work in life has to do with an absence of love."

I agreed. As I looked at the ways many people and most politicians treated each other, it seemed clear we had an absence of compassion and kindness. (Note to those calling me a Hollywood lefty right now: Compassion and kindness are not partisan issues, especially when you think about a kid showing up to school hungry or you yourself are stuck on the side of the road.)

But as an optimist with decades of therapy, support groups, and close friendships, I had hope. I believed things worked out if you leaned into the problem rather than turned away. I knew the progress that could be made when people put aside their differences, rolled up their sleeves, and got to work. When I held our chicks in my hand and felt their little hearts beating, I felt a sense of responsibility to feed and care for them. I felt the same way when I held my children and grandchildren as newborns. I may not have always taken the best care of myself, but I knew the good life was only possible when we took care of each other.

One morning in early August, the baby deer whose friendship I had nurtured since the spring ate from my hand. For some reason, I sensed that she was ready to take this final step. I held out a handful of deer corn. Instead of staying back and dropping it on the ground as I usually did, this time I kept it in my extended hand and said my good morning to her while keeping perfectly still. She looked me straight in the eyes before taking two tentative but trusting steps forward and nibbling the sweet treat.

The interaction lasted less than a minute, but I knew the connection was there for a lifetime. To me, it epitomized what was lacking or had been severely undermined in the rest of the world—trust.

Unfortunately, this was the end of this close relationship. I knew it might be wrong after traveling all this way, but I was freaked out about Lyme disease. It flourished during the summer months, and we were in peak summer. And because the mosquitos thought of my fair flesh as a three-star Michelin restaurant, I had every reason to believe they had provided glowing Yelp reviews to the ticks in the neighborhood. So, alas, I could no longer allow my deer and her tick passengers to come close to our house . . . at least not until the weather cooled exponentially.

On a much nicer note, daily life was not at all bleak. Tim and I made friends with the caretaker of the lake across the street and he invited us to go fishing with him. It was all catch and release, and fun. Right away we started thinking of reasons to go fishing there in the afternoons. After a few times, we quit looking for reasons and just went fishing.

Pretty soon, though, we ditched the fishing gear in lieu of a swim. The August humidity, while responsible for our lush gardens, was thick and draining. But only to us humans. The zinnias in our garden grew like they had been fed steroids. This was a problem—but a good one. Tall, thick, and full of flowers, they blocked the sun from a section of the vegetables. I cut a bushel's worth every week; our little Cabbage overflowed with their vibrant pinks, reds, and white, and looked like a florist's shop.

The tomatoes were another happy problem. Three weeks earlier we'd had a lot of them. Now we had even more. Way too many, in fact. I made every tomato dish in my repertoire, including tomatoes and buffalo mozzarella, fried green tomatoes, tomato panzanella salad, and tomato bisque. I sliced and quartered tomatoes on every salad we made. We diced tomatoes into our scrambled eggs. And we lunched on plain tomatoes, sliced, lightly salted, and drizzled with some balsamic vinegar, which, Tim and I both agreed, was like eating dessert.

I was ready for a tomato-based Quickfire Challenge on *Top Chef*.

"Lunchtime!" I shouted one day, before placing two gorgeous plates on the table outside and describing the dish as if I were serving Padma Lakshmi. "Grilled Halloumi cheese from Tonjes Farm with tomato and oregano from our garden, olive oil drizzle, Maldon salt, and fresh-ground pepper."

And the judge's verdict?

Deeeeeelicious!

I also made a lot of tomato sandwiches. Of all the various dishes I made, these were hands-down the winner because of the combination of ingredients.

That pinch of sugar is the magic. Seriously. If this sandwich doesn't make your tongue jump out of your face and slap you on the back of your head, I'll eat my hat.

Tomato Sandwiches

Fresh country bread, sliced thick	Thickly sliced ripe tomatoes
	Salt to taste
Butter (preferably homemade)	Freshly ground pepper to taste
Mayonnaise (preferably homemade)	Granulated sugar

Lightly toast the bread until golden. Slather one slice of bread with butter; slather another slice with mayonnaise. Place the buttered slice butter side up on a plate. Stack with sliced tomatoes. Add salt and pepper to taste. Sprinkle with a pinch of sugar. Close the sandwich with the second slice of bread, mayonnaise side down.

I really love to cook. It is my favorite creative endeavor as I get to reap the rewards by watching my food nourish my loved ones. I can cook almost everything. I say "almost" because I seemed to be the only person in America who was not able to make sourdough. I tried Mark Bittman's simple no-knead sourdough from the *New York Times*. I also tried the even simpler no-knead bread from Jim Lahey of Sullivan Street Bakery. I was told both were foolproof, something that only one in ten people can't do successfully. Well, I was the fool, the one in ten who failed.

I thought it might be the altitude. Then I attributed it to an act of God. What else could it be? I had prayed for help to stay away from the bread I had consumed for emotional comfort during lockdown, and I guess the all-knowing and loving She/He/They up there heard me. I was surprised that out of all the things I had prayed for in my life—world peace, health and happiness for everyone, the end of disease and wars, the eradication of cancer, a winning lotto ticket that went hand in hand with a promise to be very charitable—this was the one that got answered. It seemed trivial. But okay, I was glad to know my prayer had been heard.

Tim and I were eating lighter, more farm-to-table, anyway. Sure, we had indulgent Fry-days and cheeseburger Sundays, which gave us an opportunity to put slices of our gorgeous tomatoes between the buns (God was resting that day, and I was back on bread). Otherwise we enjoyed more plant-based meals where many of the ingredients came directly from our garden. Eating that way let us feel healthier, more connected to the effort we had made to grow the food, and more appreciative of nature's generosity.

It was fun. I made my own butter and pasta. We became regulars at the weekly farmer's market in Barryville. We bought our produce, meat, and cheeses from local farmers and producers, who appreciated the support. We also enjoyed knowing where our food came from. I enjoyed knowing the farmers and their families and asking them what was new and ripe. I also got their tips for cooking veggies. It was a connection I never had when hurrying through the grocery store in the city, and it deepened the gratitude I had for what I was eating.

At first, because of COVID, we placed our orders online and drove up, said our hellos, and our bags were placed in our trunk. But as we became more aware of how the virus was transmitted and how to protect ourselves from it, more vendors opened and we were able to pick the produce ourselves. We squeezed fruit and touched veggies and asked each other how things were going. Families returned. Kids and dogs ran around. Musicians played bluegrass. It was nice . . . almost normal . . . and kinder. All of us were going through something together, and even though most of our face was covered by a mask, we were glad to see one another.

One weekend Tim and I manned a table to register voters. "Step right up and find out what Michael Landon was really like," Tim barked to passersby. "And register to vote!"

"Yes, register to vote," I said, waving at people.

Because we were wearing masks, no one knew who we were. Our smiles were hidden. Everyone's smiles were hidden. We were smizing—smiling with our eyes. If you believe a person's eyes are a window into their soul, what a wonderful, remarkable thing we were sharing with each other. A smile can be faked. A soul tells all. And after months of quarantine, I was so willing and eager to share. But I noticed my crow's-feet were going bananas as a result. I was smizing so hard to ensure that people knew I was smiling at them from behind my mask that I believed I was carving lines into my face. I wondered if I should stop smiling. Was it worth it? I mentioned this dilemma to Tim, who said, "Is that really what's causing the crow's-feet?"

"Seriously, Timothy Clark?" I replied. "Now you're going to talk about my crow's-feet?"

"It wouldn't be due to growing up in the sunshine of Southern California and being over the age of fifty, would it?" he said.

"Over the age of fifty . . . *Moi!?*" I gasped, feigning shock.

I told him that I had been talking about this with my friend Amber Tamblyn and wondered how the Botox people were communicating with masks covering their faces.

"Does anyone in Beverly Hills know how anyone else is feeling right now? If your face is frozen, if you can't smize or frown, how do you express yourself?"

Toward the middle of August, it was time to move the chicks from the kitchen outside with the other chickens. I had been socializing them in the coop, leaving them in their carrying cage so they could get used to the five older chickens and vice versa. They couldn't immediately integrate without upsetting the established pecking order. One day Tim suggested I leave them in there overnight without their cage; it was time. I agreed.

When he checked on them early the next morning, he found the four mature birds sitting comfortably on their roost and the four kids huddled together in a nesting box. I hurried out in my nightgown when he called and saw with my own eyes that everyone was just fine. Not necessarily fully integrated, but no one was bleeding, so we were off to a solid start.

About this time I turned down an opportunity to audition for a television series being shot in Canada. The producers wanted me to audition, but doing that meant that if (big if) I got the part, I would have to move to Canada for months. I wouldn't be allowed to visit home at all because of quarantine rules. Tim would soon be filming his show *For Life* in New York City and would not be able to come visit me because of quarantine rules. The prospect of our being separated for months was daunting, to say the least. Particularly during the time of turbulence we were living through.

After many discussions with Tim, the decision was made and I did not do the audition. "Did you turn down this audition in Canada because we'd be apart for months on end or because you don't trust me with the chickens?"

I laughed.

But Tim's concern might have been deserved. Everyone who knew me understood that I enjoyed and needed a certain measure of control. It wasn't that I always wanted or needed to be in charge. I just felt more comfortable when I was. I suffered from what I jokingly term *competentitis*—meaning I was good and often extremely competent at a whole lot of things, maybe even most things.

Tim teased me about this one day, and, as is typical of me, I said, "I blame my mother." But I meant it as a compliment. My mother had raised me and my sister, Sara, in a way that gave us agency. We grew up feeling empowered to do anything—and I think our track record speaks for itself. This was not common among girls back in the seventies and eighties. But thanks to my mom, I came out of *Little House* with my own production company and a plan that led me to not only star in but produce the movies *The Miracle Worker* and *The Diary of Anne Frank*, among others. And when I went off on location for the first time, to Texas, where

I shot the movie *Sylvester*, the story of a sixteen-year-old orphan who, while raising her two younger brothers, turns a wild horse into a champion that she sells to the US Olympic team, I fearlessly learned to ride.

I trained four to six hours a day for months on this giant horse who periodically took off in a full run toward the woods at the end of the pasture where we rode. Either he was trying to escape or kill me or both. At first, I hung on for dear life. Then I hung on and screamed at him to stop. After a handful of these episodes, the horse realized I wasn't going away no matter how fast or far he ran, and eventually I learned how to exert control. I'd drop a rein, grab one rein with both hands, and yank his nose back into my knee. It slowed him down and started him crow-hopping, which allowed me to jump the hell off. Tim was impressed.

"What's the key to driving a covered wagon?" he asked, kidding.

"Remember your turn signals?" I laughed.

"Is there anything you can't do?" he asked.

"Oh yeah, plenty."

I scratched my head in thought. I had grown up being encouraged to try everything without worrying about failure. You can't get onstage or go in front of a camera if you are concerned about failure. In rehearsals, everyone flubs their lines. Taking the leap from real life into make-believe is the only way to find the details and mannerisms that create character; it's the only way to find out if you are any good and then to get better, and you don't get there without making mistakes. But that's true about everything, not just acting. I ended up a woman in her mid-fifties who could throw a spiral that would impress Tom Brady, bat righty or lefty, build a chicken coop, and assemble a circular saw. It resulted in a funny admission from Tim, who said, "I may have the anatomy to be the man in the family. But I am not."

"That's not accurate," I said.

"That's a nice thing to say," he responded. "But you are better with the tools, are you not?"

"Yes, I am."

"And putting things away."

"And putting things *back* where they belong—not that that's a male thing," I said.

"Wow, that went a little deeper than I thought," he said, rubbing his whiskery chin and pondering this charge before asking, "What do I leave out the most?"

"It's not one thing," I said. "You have a pile problem."

"A pile problem, you say."

"Yes, I do say." I laughed.

"I wonder what that means," he said. "What does that say about me?"

"It says you don't put things away. You let them pile up. But, as you know, I recently purchased those little baskets. So when the piles get to be too much, I move the pile into the basket and close the basket, so it's not as unsightly."

"Huh, clever."

"By the way, you're going to have to go through some of the baskets soon. They're getting pretty full. I've seen pen caps, batteries . . . lyrics to songs you've been writing. Stuff like that."

"I'm more organized than I've been in my life," Tim said. "I love you for not making me feel bad about any of this, though

I have noticed there are certain things you just won't pick up.
You'll just leave them there."

"Sometimes it's an experiment to see how long you will leave
them there," I said, grinning. "Like a used cup."

"You mean my cup for when I play baseball?" he asked.

"No, no, no." I cracked up. "A used coffee cup."

"Oh, I thought you meant—"

"Honey, please."

"Well, I did notice you made a stinky face when you moved
them around."

I give myself credit for being a very capable woman. My mother
gets credit, too. Believing myself to be capable of many things, if
not almost anything, has given me a sense of independence and
self-confidence, even at my most insecure, and that belief has kept
me afloat through tough times and provided me with a generally
positive outlook. One day when it was raining and I was in a bit of a
reflective mood (thank you very much, pandemic), I made a list of
things I know how to do, and as silly as that might sound, it made
me feel good, like I have done something with my life, like I haven't
been afraid to try. It also made me eager to add to the list.

Things I Know How to Do

✦ Tell a joke.

✦ Juggle—during my senior year of high school, our teacher,
   Coach Burr, gave us extra credit if we learned to juggle.
   Ever the overachiever, I asked my pal and prom date,
   Michael Landon Jr., who knew how to juggle, to teach me—
   and he did.

- Make amazing fried chicken.
- Paint the crap out of a paint-by-numbers kit.
- Play the Beatles' entire "Golden Slumbers/Carry That Weight/The End" medley on drums . . . including Ringo's solo.
- Get married—I learned from some real pros, and for me, the third time is the charm.
- Surf.
- Throw a perfect spiral.
- Tour the country in a musical for nine months with a broken back.
- Hit multiple bull's-eyes with my crossbow.
- Run for Congress—one of these days I may win!
- Negotiate a $200,000,000 collective bargaining agreement.
- Do a one-woman show in a theater in the West Village—it was called *My Brilliant Divorce* by Geraldine Aron, directed by my friend Aedin Moloney for her Fallen Angel Theatre Company, and it was the most challenging experience I've ever had as an actor.
- Throw a Frisbee like a champ.
- Use a table saw and a circular saw.
- Build a chicken coop.
- Put up an electric fence.
- Scare off a bear.
- Assemble any toy, piece of furniture, stereo (when those existed)—anything. I read the instructions and love putting things together.

- ✦ Handle an emergency—this is a skill I've had my whole life, whether it was when my sister had a gnarly gash in her finger, my brother had thorns embedded in his leg, or my kids broke bones or needed stitches. For some reason, I'm very calm under pressure. Once it's all over, though, I fall apart.
- ✦ Go back to school to get a degree in nursing (a dream I intend to fulfill in this lifetime).
- ✦ Find a place of real love and understanding in my heart for those with whom my past has been prickly.
- ✦ Hang out with my ex-husbands without it being the least bit weird.

Inspired by this, I emailed a few people, told them what I was up to on this rainy day, and asked them to contribute. Many sweet messages came back, but it was the one from my mother that had the most meaning for me:

- ✦ You knew how to sneak in and out of your bedroom, which apparently I didn't know until I found the broken, bent screen still in the window when we moved so many years later. 😄 😄
- ✦ The time you cut off half your hair, maybe you were 2. Put major grease in it. Vaseline or face cream. Maudie had to wash your hair w Tide or whatever we used then, and we had to get you a precious Mia Farrow haircut. 😄 😄 😄
- ✦ Hiding animals I never knew we had. 😄

- ✦ Taking over Madame Lepko's dance recital. Telling everyone they were wrong, pushing them into place. 😄
- ✦ At probably 12yrs old preparing a full Mexican dinner, decorating table etc. when we had an unexpected guest coming.
- ✦ At every commercial audition, telling the director the product was your favorite thing in the world.
- ✦ Running into an audition where the director was sitting on the floor w a group of children & throwing your arms around his neck & kissing him on the cheek. Maybe you were 3.
- ✦ The family fashion show in Hawaii, you were probably 2, we walked nicely & when we stepped down you broke away & ran back up & walked alone, posing.
- ✦ Same trip, Daddy was making a TV appearance and while we were waiting you broke away from us, ran up to a TV camera & started wildly dancing. My old brain 🧠 will undoubtedly think of more. 💀

  —Barbara Gilbert-Cowan (aka my mom)

Everything Is Everything. What Is Meant to Be Will Be.

I broke a tooth. Again. Because I'm a glamorous Hollywood star . . .

It was Sunday, and Tim and I were at the Barryville farmer's market, where we ran into a few old friends: a lobster roll, just-shucked oysters, and freshly steamed clams. All were offered by a vendor who stuffed a soft, buttery brioche with a generous portion of chunky lobster and served us a plate of oysters on ice and steamed buttery clams that glistened in the sunlight with the brilliance of diamonds on a swatch of black velvet. It was a sight!

We took our meals to a picnic table, where we sat down socially distanced from others and dove in with unabashed pleasure. With all the *ohhh*s and *mmm*s and *oh my God*s coming from us, it was like we were taking turns acting out that famous scene from *When Harry Met Sally*. We would have understood if someone heard us and said, "I'll have what they're having," and they would have been equally satisfied, I'm sure.

Except the last clam I ate had a grain of sand in it, and instead of moaning with pleasure, I heard a crystal clear *plink*—at least it was crystal clear in my head—and what came out of me was an alarming groan. *Uh-oh*. Knowing immediately what had happened, I stuck a finger in my mouth and felt around until I discerned which tooth was broken and how much of an emergency this was going to be.

Luckily, it wasn't right up front. No Krazy Glue necessary.

"I'm going to leave it until I can get to my dentist in the city," I told Tim with a calmness that no doubt was a relief to him, too, as it also signaled that we were staying put until we finished our lobster rolls.

A week or so later, I was back in the city to see my neurologist, whom I visited every three months for the migraines I have endured most of my life, and I squeezed in an appointment with my dentist. They had opened back up; everyone in the office was tested and masked. Despite the rising death rate from COVID across the country, there were numerous signs of the effort businesses were making to open up. Restaurants provided takeout. Some had erected eating areas outside on the sidewalk or in parking lots. Stores were open. Signs on their windows said, MASKS REQUIRED.

I sensed the stress of a city and its residents trying to hang on. They weren't trying to figure it out; that was too much. It seemed people were waiting for the storm to pass. I walked through Central Park and saw couples and families picnicking. Friends tossed a Frisbee. I also saw the requisite joggers and bicycle riders, all masked, of course. Those who could afford it were ditching the city and moving into the country, even beyond the Hudson Valley and the Catskills, up into the Berkshires and as far away as Vermont and Maine, hoping to escape the virus and find the small-town, back-to-basics simplicity that Tim and I had at the Cabbage.

The *New York Times* characterized the country as being in a battle against the virus and fear. Back in my beloved California, the state was being ravaged top to bottom by wildfires that stood out as being as ominously symbolic as they were destructive. The middle of the country was engaged in a civil war. We were eager to find out whom Democratic presidential candidate Joe Biden was going to pick as his vice presidential running mate.

It was a lot to digest on a daily if not hourly basis, and I was extremely happy to return to the Cabbage. My first stop was the chicken coop. Though I had only been gone two and a half days, I meant it when I stood in front of Cotton, Coco, Henny, Penny, the Andrews Sisters, Peep, and Dr. Fauci and said, "Hello, my friends. I missed you so much."

As I walked out to the garden the next morning, I had the same feeling I did when I returned to the *Little House* musical after taking a few days off to have an epidural for my not-yet-properly-diagnosed broken back. I loved this role. Slipping into my overalls had been a small pleasure that put a smile on my face. I cut zinnias and brought in an armful of pungent greenery: celery, basil, oregano, thyme, and sage. I trimmed the herbs into tiny clusters, set them in ice cube trays filled with olive oil, and froze them for use later on.

"Timmy, look at my herb bombs," I said.

"Nice," he said. "And wow, that's a lot of celery."

I nodded. "We're going to be eating a lot of peanut butter and cream cheese."

Actually, we were also doing our share to support local restaurants. Not incidentally, some of these August days and nights were so humid that it was impossible to think about standing in a hot kitchen, so not only did we want to go out, we would simply look at each other and say, "I can't." "Neither can I. Let's pick something up." I think we also just wanted to get in the car and crank up the air-conditioning, which we didn't have in the house. We went to Cedar Rapids, the Stickett Inn, Il Castello, Clancy's Diner, Back to Bakers, or BVH Sports Bar in Barryville; the Heron or the Laundrette in Narrowsburg; Henning's Local in Cochecton; the Corner or the Piazza in Eldred; and the Forestburgh General Store in Forestburgh, where the sandwiches filled my eyes with tears of joy.

Something about biting into a fresh turkey sandwich with coleslaw and Russian dressing made me weepy. We got emotional just reading the menu: "The Italian Combo—ham cappi, mortadella, salami, provolone, lettuce, tomato, onion, O+V, hot or sweet peppers." Right? So simple, yet so delicious.

We stopped to pick up food one day from the Laundrette in Narrowsburg, as a treat to ourselves before Tim went back to work. They didn't have outdoor seating yet, only takeout, but we took our food to a cute park with picnic tables around the corner. I had the pizza with spicy soppressata, tomato sauce, mozzarella, and hot honey drizzle, which is one of my favorite dishes in the world. The combination of spicy and sweet flavors was and is . . . STUPID!

For Life was the first TV series to go back into production in New York. Back in June, ABC had renewed it for a second season and started working on how to film during the pandemic. I had also been reading that Broadway might try to reopen and film and television production might resume, all tentatively and carefully, of course, but then it became clear that theater, which needed an audience, was not coming back for a long time. However, *For Life* pushed forward, and on August 26, everyone tiptoed back to work.

Tim put on a brave face as we drove into the city. I was going with him for the first week. Our friend Fawn Schneider's daughter, Savannah, had agreed to care for the chickens and the garden while I was away. Tim had been on several Zooms regarding safety protocols and received numerous emails updating procedures. Everybody got tested. Their temperatures were taken. The crew was masked and shielded. Each set was sterilized overnight and then sealed. If the seal was broken before production the next day, they were going to cancel that day's work on that particular set.

The actors didn't have to be on set all day every day, so in terms of exposure they had it easier than the crew, who were there all day. From what Tim told me, the biggest change was that they dispensed with blocking, meaning there was virtually no rehearsal; they just went in, talked through the scene, and shot.

As a result, the days ended up being very short. The actors had to be ready. There wasn't a lot of fumbling around and figuring out nuances. What struck me more than anything was the testing. Until then, Tim and I had not had any reason to get tested. We had been masked, distanced, and washing our hands as if participating in a nationwide competition for the cleanest hands in the USA. We redefined MAGA—Make America Germ-free Again. But Tim got tested two days before he went on set and again every day before shooting, as did everyone involved in the show. A nurse was hired full-time to administer the tests, and a system was put in place for contact tracing in the event it was needed.

Everything seemed to work and production went smoothly. Tim exchanged his brave face for a more normal expression lightly powdered with concern. He was and is that well balanced. However, at about the two-week mark, in mid-September, he got an unexpected call from the set. I watched his facial expression change dramatically; he looked really worried. After he hung up he turned to me and said, "We're shutting down."

"What?" I was too surprised to get the unspoken message. "You're shutting down?"

"I'm staying home," he said. "Apparently a few people tested positive but they may be false positives; they're retesting everyone, and in the meantime we are shutting down."

"For how long?"

"Don't know yet."

I scratched my head, detective-like. "Who tested positive? Do you know?"

Tim shook his head. "Nope. HIPAA rules say we can't know that."

We banked on the contact tracing's working. If Tim had been exposed to any of the people, he would get a call from the health department and the show. Over the weekend, we heard that the second tests had all been negative, but out of an abundance of caution the show was suspending production for two weeks while they figured out what was going on. So we just hunkered down at the Cabbage. With two weeks to hang out, why not?

Fall was coming. I could see it in the change of color at the very tops of the trees. For the most part, the weather was still quite warm, but I supposed the shorter days and cooler temperatures in the evenings were working their magic. I was excited for fall because up near us the colors of the fall foliage were a sight to behold. People would drive from all around to see, photograph, and marvel at the beauty that is fall in the Catskills. That year was going to be very different because, though we didn't know it yet, the country was heading into a deadly COVID surge.

Timmy and I took full advantage of those glorious early fall days. One day we decided to take a drive with the sunroof open and the car windows down, while we reveled in the picturesque scenery. The drive proved a good distraction from worrying about whether Tim had been exposed and the two of us were now part of a chain of infection. Once we hit SR 17B, the road was wide open and we were feeling positive, hopeful, and hungry. We stopped for sandwiches in Bethel at Bethel Market Cafe, another good distraction. As we sat outside and ate, Tim's phone rang. He checked the caller ID and I saw his expression change.

"What?" I said sharply.

"The ID says 'NYC COVID 19,'" he said. "I gotta answer it."

"Yes, you do."

After saying hello, Tim listened intently and I could hear every word. The caller explained that she was part of the contact tracing team. She said Tim had come in contact with one of the people who had tested positive. (We traded alarmed looks across the table.) But she quickly added that they thought it was likely a false positive because of the second tests. (Looks of relief.) She wouldn't tell Tim who had tested positive, falsely or otherwise, but she said that if this person or persons tested positive again he would have to get tested again, too.

The news was neither bad nor good. Sometimes the day rests on whether you see the glass as half-empty or half-full. Both Tim and I saw the glass as three-quarters full. We had been super careful and responsible, so we trusted the odds were in our favor. No one in my circle of family or friends had been infected—not the relatives, kids, or grandkids.

Tim and I stepped back into our daily routines. He worked on his scripts, and I buried my nose in books and articles about race, equity, and diversity, trying to figure out the truth of who we really are and how we can get to where I think we need to be in order to be educated, equal, and enlightened.

Another interesting phenomenon began to happen: Every time Tim or I sniffled, sneezed, felt out of sorts, had a spasm of indigestion, suffered a moment of congestion, or thought we weren't tasting our food properly, we assumed the worst—*COVID!* A very strange state of being for two non-alarmist, non-hypochondriacal people.

We were always able to quickly talk ourselves off the cliff. Occasionally we even laughed at ourselves. Paranoia itself was an insidious virus. We knocked on wood quite a bit, enough that my knuckles developed a sensitivity. Then Tim came down with a stomach thing. At that point intestinal distress was one of the symptoms. So when he felt a little clammy, I made him soup and took his temperature, which was normal, and tucked him into bed.

Tim was still under the weather a few days later, so he went for a COVID test. We were both very worried. Then Timmy called me from the road and we had a conversation that I knew tens of thousands of people all over the world were having.

Timmy said, "What if I'm positive?"

This idea filled me with a terror I hadn't felt since the day my youngest son was born nearly three months early.

We talked about whether he should come back to the Cabbage or go stay away from me in the apartment. I was shaking uncontrollably and on the verge of tears as we discussed the logistics of what a positive result would mean. Then Timmy said, "I need to check my will. Make sure it's completely up to date." That sentence pushed me over the edge. With tears now pouring down my cheeks I said, "Baby, let's cross that bridge if and only if we get to it, please."

He arrived at the testing place and before we hung up I said, "We will deal with this, whatever it is, and we will be okay. I love you."

"I love you, wife," he said.

All there was to do then was wait.

My brain was racing. What if, what if, what if . . . What might he need? Where would it be best for him to be, in the city with access to the big, fancy, but horribly overcrowded hospitals, or up at the Cabbage with access to smaller ones? Was I going to stay with him or in whichever place was empty? I didn't see how I could be away from him. I did not acquire my formidable nursing skills to turn away my husband in his hour of need. I would also have to call the kids and his siblings and his bestie Casey, run point if he needed more acute care, and so on.

Twenty minutes later Tim called; his rapid-test results had come back negative. All of that pacing and heart-fluttering worry had been for naught. Though it gave us both a teeny-tiny taste of what far too many people were going through around the world. My heart ached for those dealing with this horrible virus in a new and deeper way. Our brush with the possibility of COVID-19 had made us even more sensitive to the plight of those facing it every day.

It had also turned out that the test results that had shut down production were all false positives. Blame fell on the lab.

Once the immediate scare was over, we sat down to discuss it and decompress.

"On the plus side, despite your stomach issue, we have been incredibly healthy all year," I said. "I normally get two or three colds a year. I've had nothing so far."

"All the mask wearing and hand sanitizing," Tim said.

"I may keep wearing a mask forever," I said. "Why not?"

Tim tipped his head and looked askance at me. "Because we gotta see that famous Halfpint smile."

"Back at ya, handsome."

Tim went back to work in the city two or three days a week, depending on the episode, and I stayed in the country. I read and toiled in the garden. One day I proudly stuck a Biden-Harris sign at the end of our driveway. Those weren't so prevalent in our neck of the woods. I began to sense the debate people like me and Tim were going to have down the line as we got a handle on COVID and businesses opened up in some fashion.

What were we going to take with us as we returned to work and leisure again? What were we going to leave behind? The pundits and politicians constantly spoke about getting back to normal.

What was normal? Did such a thing even exist? Prior to COVID, Tim and I had been talking about the possibility of preparing for a climate apocalypse. Did we want to go back to where we had been? Hadn't we learned anything valuable? What changes did we want to make?

That was all TBD. But the arrival of fall underscored that, like it or not, change was constant and impervious to resistance. The air chilled. The garden thinned and plants yellowed and drooped. Having given all they had, they were exhausted, done. Days got shorter. The bugs were not as loud—or buggy. I sat in the yard one afternoon and got buzzed by one of our more recurrent hummingbirds. Our sweet little friend was mostly green, with a brown breast and a tinge of yellow, as if she had been designed by Gucci.

I felt like she was bidding me adieu, till the spring, and off to spend the winter in a warmer climate where she could nosh on wildflowers.

Tim and I headed up to the Laundrette to pick up dinner. Our favorite restaurant had one of our favorite views. We stood outside waiting for our food looking out at the Delaware River, an old bridge, and trees for as far as we could see. As the light changed, so did the reflections on the water. It was easy to feel as if we were standing inside a Frederic Church painting. A few days later, we were on our way to Port Jervis and stopped at the Hawks Nest to admire the fall colors.

Another time, at the last minute, I drove into the city to run errands but made time to stroll through Central Park, where I came upon a couple of female violinists performing a Bach *Brandenburg Concerto*. I came to the conclusion that life could be and actually was very busy while on lockdown. It could also be quite beautiful, sad, and inspiring.

I was juggling all these thoughts one afternoon as I began to figure out dinner. I looked back at the past few months and realized we had lost John Lewis, John Prine, Wilford Brimley, Chadwick Boseman, and Ruth Bader Ginsburg, along with hundreds of thousands of less heralded but no less meaningful lives lost to COVID. A few weeks earlier I had posted a picture of my father on Instagram in recognition of National Suicide Prevention Month. I had also acknowledged National Sons Day and Michael's twenty-fifth birthday, and posted an old picture I came across of me and rocker Billy Idol on a date from way back in the eighties. Now both of us were grandparents.

What the actual fuck? How did that happen?!

Maybe all the time in the country has made me more philosophical. From what I have witnessed, life happens whether we like it or not, and then it goes on without us. We have to decide what wisdom we'll share and leave behind to ensure the survival of the generations that follow. So what wisdom can we glean from a pandemic? It's a test, a pause, a time-out, the way a kindergarten teacher sends a disruptive kid into the corner to contemplate their bad or unruly behavior. We are being given an opportunity to see the consequences of our disregard for our home and each other. We are being asked what really matters. What do we need to do to survive into the future?

I know my outspokenness will upset some people. I am fine with that. At this age, I feel I've earned the right to speak up. As a seventeen-year-old, I starred in a remake of the movie *Splendor in the Grass*. It was a good idea, but I had yet to fall in love, and certainly not to the point where I was willing to give up everything I had for another human being, and thus I had no way of relating to that character. I was inauthentic. Such is not the case when I offer an opinion now. I have run for office. I have headed a union. I have negotiated contracts. I have given birth and raised children. I have walked friends through medical crises. I have buried loved ones. I have married, divorced, and remarried. I have been rich and poor. I have moved. I have gone under and bobbed back up. As I like to say, I know how to pack a suitcase.

My point? I want people to know they aren't alone. Nobody is so special that they are the only ones who have walked through something. If I can help make someone feel less isolated, scared, or lonely, I am doing my job.

The spirit of what I felt was captured in another way by Laura Ingalls Wilder, who wrote, "The real things haven't changed. It is still best to be honest and truthful; to make the most of what we have; to be happy with simple pleasures; and have courage when things go wrong." I had that in mind when I decided to make chicken tikka masala (not with our chickens) and got out a thirty-two-ounce jar of tomatoes that I had canned two months earlier. This was the first jar I opened; either it would be a simple pleasure or I would need to have courage.

I twisted the top open, bent down over the counter, and inhaled. As I breathed in the gorgeous aroma of those tomatoes, the tomatoes I had planted, nurtured, picked, and prepared, I realized that I was, in fact, breathing in everything that happened in my life. I was breathing in everything that had led me to that moment . . . and that moment was exactly, sublimely perfect.

The Incredible Edible Egg

After months of letting nature take its course, the hens were finally of age to lay eggs. There was not a person on one of our group texts who did not know the time had arrived. I knew because I had been reading the Internet as if I were studying to become an ob-gyn for chickens. *Scientia potentia est.* Knowledge is power. Although Tim put it in much friendlier language when he said simply the kids could have kids.

Indeed, most hens are about four and a half months old when they lay their first egg, and so I informed Coco, Cotton, Henny, and Penny of this one day when I had the talk with them. The talk every responsible mother has with her daughters. You girls are now women. Though eager to get our first eggs, I knew better than to pressure them, in the same way I had been aware that Dakota and Marissa were trying to get pregnant but I knew it was best not to text every day and ask how it was going. Of course, chickens are different. I didn't have to ask.

Every morning when I went out to do what I called my chicken chores—making sure they had water and food, scooping up their poop, ensuring the coop was bug-free—I peeked into their nesting box. But for all of Tim's and my anticipation, concern, patience, excitement, encouraging words, and checking, we missed the first freakin' egg!

It was early November, and we were in the city for Tim's work, my latest dental appointment, and various other errands. Since we were there, we stayed to watch the election results, which kept us up all night and then stupidly through the rest of the week. Before Joe Biden's victory was confirmed, Savannah Schneider, Fawn's daughter, who tended to the chickens while we were away, texted us a picture of a tiny brown egg. With that, Coco won the medal for first place in our egg-laying contest.

"Oh my God!" I screamed. "Timmy!"

I texted the photo to my family. *Look, we got an egg!*

The next day, Saturday, I texted everyone another photo, this one of Joe Biden, who had officially been awarded enough Electoral College votes to be declared the winner. *Look, we got a president!*

What a time we were living in!

On Sunday, Tim and I returned to the country. I was very excited that we were going to get fresh eggs. The next morning I hurried out to the coop, checked the nesting box, and found nothing. I was also disappointed when I checked that afternoon. The same thing happened the next two days. I thought, Oh great, they're going to lay eggs for Savannah but not me—and I was their mom! The next morning, however, the ladies made it up to me. Peeking into the nesting box, I spied two little eggs, one brown, and one tiny and . . . and . . . *green!*

The tininess was normal. At first eggs are tiny. As for the color, depending on the breed of chicken, they might be off-white, green, blue, or a pale yellow. They were beautiful, especially that first little green egg. I ran with them into the house, squealing with glee like it was my birthday, Christmas, and maybe the birth of my children.

"Look!" I said, holding them out for Tim to see. "A Coco egg, and from Cotton a green egg!"

"Where's the ham?" he asked.

Again, I texted everyone pictures. It was a massive accomplishment, and I hadn't done a damn thing besides offering encouragement and celebrating this big day. Down the line, after Henny, Penny, the Andrews Sisters, and Peep all began to lay eggs, giving us five or six eggs every day, I researched the best way to keep them and how long they stayed fresh. I was only accustomed to buying eggs at the grocery store, where they were already refrigerated. But I found out unwashed eggs that have never been refrigerated can be stored on the counter for between six weeks and two and a half months, depending upon the room temperature. The cooler the room, the longer they will keep. I also learned the float test. If in doubt about the freshness of an egg, place it in a cup of water. If it sinks, it is okay to eat. If it floats, trash it.

Tim and I had no such worries about our green egg. We set it and the brown egg, only hours old when I brought them into the house, on the counter, where they could be admired throughout the day and night as if they were newly unearthed crown jewels on display at a museum. The next day we had to return to the city. For the drive, I hard-boiled the brown egg and gave it to Tim as a snack. Humbled by this honor, he held the egg up in his hand as we drove and approached the first bite with reverential diligence. Both of us expected it to live up to and even surpass all those well-known slogans about eggs: Happiness is egg shaped. Egg-ceptional every day. The incredible edible egg.

Except it wasn't incredible. It was inedible. Incredibly inedible. The yolk was surrounded by a weird, thick membrane. It was awful and disgusting.

I saw Tim's face contort. He opened the window and spat it out.

"What is it?" I asked.

"Gross," he said.

"But what was it?"

He started to describe it to me but I held up my hand and then turned away while making a gagging sound.

"No! I don't want to know. I can't. One gross thing will turn me off from eating eggs forever, and I don't want to do that."

I am like that. If I find a bug or something else in my food, I won't eat that particular item for a long time. Maybe forever. (FYI, I googled gross things found in food and came upon an article on Eat This, Not That confirming my worst fears. The unexpected bits and pieces people have found in their food include a black widow spider in grapes, a condom in a Big Mac, a frog in a bag of salad, a tooth in a candy bar, and a finger in a can of chili. You don't even want to hear the story Michael Landon told me about working in a canned soup factory way back when. There's plenty more, and plenty worse. But yuck. I don't want to know.)

To ensure we didn't run into any problems with our eggs in the future, we agreed to scramble the next few. I am happy to report they surpassed expectations and redefined the way eggs tasted.

This was particularly true as time enabled the chickens to lay more eggs. As they did, the eggs got larger and richer. When we scrambled them, they were denser, more velvety, and way more flavorful. That could have been my imagination, as I treated each individual egg as an artistic expression with whose feathery provenance I had a personal connection, and each day I thanked the ladies in the coop for their gifts. "They really are yummy," I gushed.

But so much for clucking around. The rest of the month was nonstop busy. On Saturday night, I arranged a family Zoom. Dakota and Marissa had big news, though I told everyone that I wanted to give them an update on my neck surgery, which had finally been scheduled for the middle of November. Getting everyone in my family to show up someplace on time is a task itself. A Zoom chat can be even harder. It's not like I can send a car for everyone to ensure they show up, the way they do on talk shows.

The plan was for Marissa and Dakota to join late, after everyone else was already in the Zoom. They were also going to put Marissa's first ultrasound up as their background. At three o'clock Eastern time (noon West Coast time), everyone was onscreen except my sister. Sara was running late. In her defense, she had three kids and was very hands-on, especially on the weekends. I texted her. *You really need to get on this call. There's important stuff going on here that you're definitely going to want to hear.*

I'm doing the best I can, she responded.

Finally, Sara got on and I signaled Marissa and Dakota to join. When they came on, everybody was talking at once, asking me questions about my surgery. Suddenly, Sam's wife, Andrea, scrunched up her face the way people do when they are momentarily perplexed and said, "Marissa, what's that picture behind you?" She had noticed the ultrasound. Then everybody else did, too, and one by one, like the squares in *The Brady Bunch*, everyone screamed "Oh my God!" and celebrated, while my mom, who hadn't picked up on the background, asked, "What is it? What's going on?" Then she realized what the image was and started to cry. It was so us, and so happy.

A couple days later, Tim and I packed up and went to the city. I got my teeth cleaned and had my pre-op physical, and that night, the tenth, after a few hours of lounging around, we had dinner at Salumeria Rosi, a tiny Italian restaurant and *salumi* shop that we adored on nearby Amsterdam Avenue. The night was a celebration of our first date. It was also the calm before the storm that was going to be my surgery.

But first things first: Restaurants had officially been allowed to open for indoor dining. When we arrived, we were offered an indoor table. We were super reluctant and tentative but there was no one else seated inside and the restaurant had taken the mandated precautions. We talked it over and decided it was safe enough. Walking into a restaurant and being shown to a table was so damn strange. This was the first time we had taken off our masks in a public establishment with other people nearby, though the waitstaff and everyone else working there remained masked. The restaurant was small to begin with, maybe twelve or fifteen tables total, but they had pared down to about six tables, including ours, separated by Plexiglas dividers and set the requisite six feet apart. But still. How many months had we spent keeping our distance from other human beings and covering our faces to avoid airborne germs?

As we sat and talked, though, we grew more comfortable. I was feeling almost normal as I dipped a piece of fresh warm bread into a bowl of rich olive oil and speared a small chunk of Parmesan, when Tim glanced farther to his right and noticed we were seated adjacent to the restaurant's HEPA air purifier. It was a foot away from my head. Without saying a word, both of us realized all of the germs in the restaurant and perhaps this section of New York City were being sucked right past us.

We heard someone in the back of the restaurant sneeze. I wanted to duck under the table and crawl outside and back to the car. An average human sneeze can release more than one hundred thousand germ-carrying droplets traveling at over one hundred miles per hour. Picture a missile being fired off the wing of an F-15. I did not used to think this way. Maybe I had a touch of phobia in me, but that was just a basic fear of dying. It wasn't like we were living now, not when I felt my private space was being breached and my life endangered by a cough.

Arrrgh!

"Well, shit," I said.

Tim nodded. "Look, we've already been exposed to whatever germs are flying past our faces and the waiter is coming with our dinner . . . so . . . I think we should just try to enjoy dinner. Eat first. Worry later."

I was of the same opinion two days later when I read a mention of stuffing-flavored potato chips at Trader Joe's. Anyone who knows me is aware that old-fashioned, Thanksgiving-style white-bread stuffing is one of my favorite things in the world. I am not even limiting it to food; it is one of my favorite things, period. And potato chips are not far behind. I read about these stuffing-flavored chips and I thought, We are in the midst of a pandemic, I am about to fly to Los Angeles, and I am having spinal surgery. All three are risky ventures. Life is short. Life is precarious. I am not going to die, God forbid, without at least tasting stuffing-flavored potato chips, or even eating an entire bag . . . myself!

Was this something lockdown had done to my brain? I doubt it. I think I would have come to this conclusion pandemic or no pandemic. I mean, stuffing-flavored potato chips!

I ordered them immediately. When they arrived, I stopped whatever I was doing, sat down, and opened a bag. I breathed in the aroma from the bag as one might do a bottle of fine wine. I was immediately drunk with anticipation. But I cautioned myself to be-have. Willpower, I said. Only have one or two chips. The first one was pure OMG. After the second one, I whimpered, "What kind of magic is this?"

If I weren't married to Tim, I would have eloped with those chips. I couldn't wait to share them with Tim. When he got home from work, I practically shoved the bag at him.

"You have to," I said. "These are life-changing."

A good sport, he bit into a chip, turned it around in his mouth as he chewed, and gave me a tiny head shake.

"I don't love 'em," he said.

"You don't?" I asked, aghast.

"Not so much," he said.

"I *love* them," I said. "I really love them."

He shrugged. "Okay, but I pass."

"You pass?"

"Yeah, they aren't my bag."

"They're my bag . . . all my bag, and they're stupid," I said.

For someone who was having spinal surgery in a few days, I was unusually calm. I think all the planning I had to do to get to California provided a sense of control, as well as a distraction. It was not simple. Dr. Bray was operating in his Newport Beach surgical facility, and because Tim was working, I had to fly solo. Going west, I needed to take every possible precaution short of wrapping myself in plastic to avoid exposure to COVID. If I even had a slight temperature, the procedure would be canceled. Then I had to get back to New York post-surgery, with no one carrying my bag and my being unable to put anything in the overhead bin or under the seat without help, and still avoid the damn virus.

As I discussed this with family and friends, everyone's first suggestion was to fly private, as if we had access to a private jet. Even if we did, the cost was prohibitive; one-way was about thirty thousand dollars. Such travel fell under the old adage "If you have to ask the price, you can't afford it." I ended up using all of my airline miles to book a first-class ticket on American. I hadn't traveled for a year so I had a crazy amount.

"Getting this surgery planned and scheduled has taken the same length of time it took Coco and Cotton to grow from chicks to hens and lay their first egg," I said to Tim one day.

"Huh, I didn't realize that," he said.

"Do you think there's a connection?"

Tim tried not to laugh. "Uh, no."

On November 16, I got on my flight at JFK, wearing my mask, rubber gloves, and plastic face shield, and I wiped down my seat and everything around me with Clorox wipes before settling in with my magazines and water bottle. I wasn't going to eat or drink anything on the plane, but the flight attendants were also masked and gloved and taking every precaution, the same as me, so about thirty minutes into the flight I thought, Why not have the meal and some hot tea while I watch a movie?

Halfway across the country, though, at about the same time I was thinking this wasn't so terrible, the pilot came on the intercom and said something like, "Ladies and gentlemen, we are getting a reading on our fuel gauges that we don't like, so we are going to land at the nearest airport and get this taken care of." At first, I thought of my mother, who, unlike me, is terrified of flying. This would have killed her. It sent me into hyper-thought, my mind racing through as many possibilities as I could imagine.

What did the pilot mean? Were we leaking fuel? Were we able to land? Were we landing out of proper caution or was this an emergency? And what degree of emergency was this? Should I be making a goodbye-I-love-you video on my phone and texting it to Tim and the kids?

I signed on to the Gogo in-flight Internet and texted updates to Tim: We were landing in Tulsa. The pilot warned us that we were going to see a lot of emergency vehicles on the runway watching us land.

Don't panic, Tim said.

That's what the pilot told us, I replied.

Trust him, Tim texted. *He doesn't want to die, either. Watch the flight attendants. If they stay calm, you can stay calm.*

He just said that we are going to stop on the runway. If there's an issue, they will evacuate the plane. If not, they will pull up to the gate and figure out what's going on with the gauge.

Sounds good.

Oy.

We landed and stopped on the runway, and sure enough, like in the movies, I saw a phalanx of yellow fire trucks and ambulances idling nearby. Everyone was very calm. I was visualizing what I would do if we had to jump off the plane. Would I take my stuff or leave it? Before I made up my mind, the pilot announced we were moving to an empty gate. No one had to jump off the plane today. The fuel gauge was indeed faulty, but rather than fix it there, they literally put some kind of measuring stick in the fuel tank, checked the result, and after a roughly two-hour delay, we were back in the air. The pilot, crew, and ground crew were impressive.

I had intended to pick up a rental car at LAX after landing, drive to Newport, and get an MRI, X-ray, and CT scan so Dr. Bray could study a fresh set of images before the surgery. By this time, however, we were running about three hours behind schedule. From the air, I communicated with my longtime travel agent, Stephen Miny, who arranged for a car to pick me up instead. *I need a speed racer*, I told him. Thankfully, the imaging center stayed open late for me and whisked me through after I finally arrived, breathless and grateful.

At a certain point in my life, I would have been exhausted from stress and freaking out about all those added hours. But a combination of age, therapy, and Baba had helped me. I still tried to bend situations to my will, but if, after five minutes, that didn't work, which had been the case on the plane, I thought, Maybe I am supposed to sit on this plane for another three hours, read my book, watch a movie, and ask for more cookies.

The silver lining in all this was the opportunity to spend the next couple of days with my best friend in the whole world, Sandy Peckinpah. After months in quarantine, I had forgotten what it was like to be with a best friend—specifically, a best girlfriend. I was married to my other best friend. Though I had Zoomed with Sandy during the past year, it was an altogether different experience to see her pull up in front of my hotel and hug her. We literally ran toward each other.

When we both said, "I missed you," we were talking about each other and so much more. But it was really about us, our friendship, our connection. God, how much I had missed that experience of being in person. This was what COVID did to all of us. We were deprived of being with family and friends. A video chat was not the same as when I got into Sandy's car and said, "After we get our COVID tests, let's go to Whole Foods." Which was what we did. Our rapid tests came back negative. Then we picked up the food I would need after surgery because the facility's café was closed. And then we had lunch at my hotel's restaurant, where we sat looking out at Newport Bay. The spicy fried chicken sandwiches we ordered were sublime. The sun was out, and the day was gorgeous. Seventy degrees in the middle of November. This was the way Southern California seduced people.

That afternoon I had a pre-op meeting with Dr. Bray, who discussed the procedure with me. He said my latest MRI images confirmed what he'd expected but also showed a little more damage than he had anticipated. In a worst-case scenario, he would have to fuse the vertebrae together. If I woke up from the operation without a collar, it would mean that he was able to avoid the fusion and put in an artificial disc. That became my mantra the rest of that day and night when I checked in with Tim and the kids: *Let's wake up without a collar.*

Spending time with Sandy was a big deal. We had been friends for thirty-plus years. Our mutual friend Jack Scalia had introduced us, and it was love at first sight. We have been through divorces, separations, weddings, births, and funerals. We walked together through the unexpected and heart-shattering death of her firstborn son, Garrett. We walked through the deaths of my grandfather and grandmother. We did the same with the passing of her ex, David. Sandy is the one person other than Tim with whom I am able to pick up the phone and say, "I need you," and she'll come running. I know she feels the same way about me. The trust and support that comes with such a friendship is truly indispensable, and COVID had denied us so much of what we relied on together.

Sandy had volunteered to spend this time with me, driving me wherever and doing whatever I needed, and also just hanging out. I said yes a bit reluctantly. I knew she was going through a lot of stuff at the time, literally up to her eyeballs in all things kids, family, husband, and the pandemic, and the last thing I wanted to do was burden her with something else. But putting her life on pause for two days actually allowed her the time to unburden herself. It gave her a moment of escape from everything else.

I understood. Life is not always about you, even when you think it's about you. This is the beauty of friendship. We had dinner together that night and talked and caught up while eating great food and sitting by the ocean. In the midst of this time when no one could see anyone in person, this was a blessing.

And not the only one. Early the next morning, I showered and packed. Sandy drove me to Dr. Bray's facility and sat with me in pre-op. I texted with Tim and my children the whole time, practically nonstop; our group chain was an ongoing conversation. When I wrote that I was heading into surgery in about twenty minutes, everyone responded instantly. My phone pinged and chirped like a Vegas slot machine hitting the jackpot. They loved me, they said, and knew the procedure was going to go well. As I lay there drowning in heart emojis, Dakota's wife, Marissa, added, *It better go well. Your GRANDDAUGHTER is going to need you.*

That was their way of revealing the gender to the entire family, and it could not have gone over better. "It's a girl!" I screamed to Sandy, who added her own joyous scream, which brought the nurses hurrying into the room, and then they added their voices to the chorus of excitement. By then, I imagined the harbormaster in the nearby marina must have also heard the news. I turned to Sandy and said, "How can I feel anything but hope for the future?"

I was calm as they started my IV. Dr. Bray and his nurses came in and out of the pre-op room as they prepped me. Everyone was chipper and chatty.

"I saw the video of Ruby Rose's surgery," I told Dr. Bray, who had performed a similar operation to mine on the *Batwoman* actress in 2019 and posted a graphic video of the surgery on his website. "I'm jealous."

"That same crew happens to be here right now," he said. "Do you want us to shoot your surgery?"

"Yes, please," I said.

After I met them, one of Dr. Bray's technicians came in and attached electrodes to my fingers, my toes, my legs, my neck, and my head. The wires had tiny pins at the tips, which were to be stuck into my skin after I was under anesthesia. As Dr. Bray opened up the nerve canals in my neck, these electrodes would show energy spikes in the areas where I had experienced numbness. It was very state-of-the-art, but all the wires and the potential pricks finally made me anxious. In a few minutes, Dr. Bray was going to cut my throat open and operate on my spine AGAIN. I was treating the surgery like it wasn't a big deal, but it was a big deal.

I turned to a nearby nurse and said, "Okay, now I'm nervous."

"We'll take care of that," she said.

The anesthesiologist came in and shot something in my IV.

"How are you feeling now?" he asked.

"Not nervous," I said.

"Comfortable?" the nurse asked.

I nodded, slipping rapidly into a sense of calm.

The next thing I knew they were wheeling me into the OR. I was moved onto the operating table while everyone buzzed around prepping me and the room. All the while, I was a little buzzed from the meds and chatting away. Finally, it was time to start and the anesthesiologist began injecting the anesthesia into my IV. I had watched a lot of medical documentaries and seen a lot of people go under anesthesia. They usually said something very profound and moving. Not me. My final words as I drifted off were not "Tell my family I love them" or "Please take care of me." Nope, my final words were, "Hey, have you guys ever tried Trader Joe's stuffing-flavored potato chips?"

Less than two hours later, I was waking up in the post-op recovery room. As usual, I metabolized the anesthesia quickly and it didn't take me long to be almost fully awake. I knew right away that I did not have a collar.

"He did it, didn't he?" I said, or rather croaked, since my throat was dry and scratchy and my voice a raspy whisper.

Sandy nodded. "You have an artificial disc."

"Hurray!"

I shut my eyes and breathed in a sort of meditative acknowledgment of the relief and gratitude I felt just then. It was easy to be a little la-la Zen. I was still a bit woozy. What nearly escaped me but then became glaringly obvious was that the constant pain I had grown used to was no longer there. It was gone. Dr. Bray walked into the room, still in his blue-green scrubs, and paused. Then he crossed to the other side of the room. I followed him with my eyes.

"You can move your head," he said.

"I can?" I said, surprised.

"In the operating room just now, we were moving your head all over the place. Up. Down. Right. Left."

"Really?"

"So look at me over here," he said. "Turn your head."

A few minutes later, they sat me in a chair and brought me a cup of crushed ice. I ate Jell-O. I called Tim and texted everyone else that I was out of surgery and already moving my head and neck. I walked to the bathroom. I drank water like I had just trekked across the desert with Peter O'Toole. I walked to the bathroom all night. The following morning, I moved in with the Brays, where I continued my recovery for the next three days.

Who doesn't want to heal at their surgeon's house? Prior to the operation, I had been teleconferencing with Dr. Bray and his assistant, Layla, about post-op logistics. I mentioned that Tim was filming and I had to figure out where I would stay. Dr. Bray leaned toward the screen and said, "You're staying with us."

"Are you sure?" I asked.

"Well, let me check with my wife," he said. "But yes, I'm sure."

This was yet another silver lining. In addition to the operation, I had been reunited with my best friend, and now I was unexpectedly being welcomed as a houseguest. During COVID! The Brays were wonderful people, and I loved hanging out and recuperating with them. They were warm, bright, and inquisitive. I was ready for conversation. They also had a five-year-old daughter, Madison, who came into my room in the mornings, hopped up on the bed, and told me fantastic tales about her stuffed animals. Sometimes a situation will strike me as familiar and I will think back to a scene or an episode of *Little House on the Prairie*, which often looms in the web of my life as a primer for all the lessons I would need to be a good person as an adult. I know I am not alone in that; I just have more of a personal connection. But this was one of those times. And as I hugged the Brays goodbye, grateful for so much beyond my new disc and liberation from pain, I heard Laura Ingalls Wilder in my head: "It is not the things you have that make you happy. It is love and kindness and helping each other and just plain being good."

On November 23, just four days after surgery, I was winging

my way back east. On the plane and in the car that picked me up at JFK, I pinched myself and blissfully felt every nerve in my body respond—no numbness, a little post-op pain but nothing like the pain I'd been living with for decades, no more limitations. It was a miracle. But I wasn't as confident about my exposure to COVID with this cross-country travel. To be on the safe side, Tim decamped to the Cabbage, leaving me to recoup for four days in the apartment. Michael came by to help me unpack and settle in.

Tim had picked up an entire Thanksgiving feast from our local gourmet grocery store and put it in the fridge. It was just for me. On Thursday, all I had to do was heat up the turkey, stuffing, and green beans, and voilà, before I could figure out whether the Pilgrims were woke or on the list to be canceled, I was enjoying my meal, talking on the phone with Tim, and texting the rest of my crew all the reasons we had to be grateful even though we were spending this particular Thanksgiving apart.

"How are the chickens?" I asked Tim.

"Good," he said. "How are you?"

"Pain-free," I said.

"Amazing."

"Good night, husband."

"Good night, wife."

I hung up and texted the kids,

Good night, Wammer.

Good night, Mel.

Good night, Rocket.

Good night, Mel.

Good night, Leezer Peezer Lemon Squeezer.

Good night, Mel.

Good night, Miss Missa.

Good night, Peesh.

Good night, Firstborn.

Good night, Mother.

Good night, Peeker McSqueak.

Good night, Ma.

I turned my phone off, settled into bed, and realized that we had turned into a modern version of the Waltons.

Hope Is the Dream
of a Waking Woman

It was morning in early January, and Michael, who had spent Christmas and New Year's with us and had no plans to depart, stood in the kitchen in a white T-shirt and baggy sweats with his freshly washed hair wrapped in a towel. This was the breakfast rush, Gilbert-Busfield style. As Michael contemplated how many eggs he wanted to scramble, he was distracted by something out the window that caught his eye. A moment later, he yelled, "Ma, Little is out there looking for you."

I shut my laptop, walked into the kitchen, grabbed a handful of apples from a large bag on the counter, and glanced out the window. There was Little, a baby deer with a mangled right front leg. She was standing in the backyard, waiting for me to bring her some food, as was our routine.

I threw a down parka over my flannel jammies and stepped outside. I approached Little slowly, greeting her softly: "Good morning, how are you today?" I might have also informed her about the latest shenanigans coming out of the White House, though I could tell that she wasn't as interested or outraged as I was about the Michael Flynn pardon. Her eyes were trained on the apples in my hand.

"Good girl," I said. "You look beautiful today."

Her nose twitched.

We had met late last fall during that period when sweater weather had yielded to colder temperatures and heavy jackets. The grass was gone and the pretty paint-by-number colors on the leaves had been replaced by a dreary assortment of browns and bare branches. I had quit feeding the deer because of the ticks and my fear of Lyme disease, and they had gone elsewhere for leaves and seeds and berries and acorns. It saved us money; I had been going through a half dozen bags of Red Delicious a day.

But the deer had recently started showing up again. As the weather changed, it was as if they remembered the friendly lady with the bags of apples and decided to do a drive-by. One day I spotted Little behind the others. She was smaller and walked with a pronounced limp. I reached for the binoculars we keep by the kitchen window for when we want to get a closer look at wildlife outside without opening the door and spooking them into flight. That's when I saw the damage to her leg. From her knee down there was nothing but bone; it wasn't bleeding but it looked raw and very painful. I figured that she'd gotten it caught in something and ripped off all the flesh trying to get her leg out.

I had grabbed a bag of deer corn, walked outside, and threw some in her direction. The other deer froze and watched me. But the injured little girl walked over to the corn and ate. She was hungry.

After that, I set food out for her. Every morning after my chicken chores, and every early evening, I made a pile of deer corn and scattered a few apples nearby. It was like I was fixing her a plate of food at a rehab facility. But why not? At the time, I was preparing for my own surgery. I understood what it meant to be in pain. Offering a helping hand was part of the unspoken agreement we had with each other when one of us was hurting, including animals. I was merely being kind and compassionate.

Okay, I was being a mom.

We named her Little Foot, which I shortened to Little, and she started visiting by herself. The more I fed her, the more she got used to me. Having been down this road before, I was patient, and so was she. Each day, we inched a bit closer until we were only about two or three feet apart. I talked to her. We looked in each other's eyes. We had a nice thing going.

Then in early December we were hit hard by several big snowfalls and I didn't see Little anymore. The snow was gorgeous. The entire outdoors was painted white. I remember going outside one day to shovel snow and being struck by rays of sun slashing through the trees. I called for Tim, wanting to share the beauty of the scene with him.

"It's proof of God," I said. "This is a God I can believe in."

"Absolutely," he agreed.

Little had no idea, but at the time Tim and I were celebrating the birth of our third grandchild, Eli Francis Ackerman. He was the second child of his daughter, Daisy. His first grandchild, Ruby Jennings Ackerman, had been born in 2018. After he got the news that she was on the way, I asked how he felt, and he beamed. "It's enchanting." This time I saw a cloud of sadness float across Tim's face as he realized we would not be able to meet this newest addition to the family right away because of COVID. All I could do was empathize. An Internet meme I saw was true—"Grandchildren make the world a little softer, a little warmer, a little kinder"—and boy, did I also miss holding a newborn.

I didn't realize it at the time, but I guess I satisfied that craving by caring for Little. She let me stand between her and the other deer while she ate. On the morning Michael saw her, she had arrived early, ahead of the pack, and come right up to the house, as if looking for the doorbell. She waited for me to come outside. When I finally appeared, apples and corn in hand, she seemed to dance in place, excited.

"Hello, Little," I said. "I'm happy to see you, too."

I was Halfpint again.

Actually, I had never stopped being Halfpint.

The holiday season could not have been happier. I was nurturing and feeding my family, all with a fire crackling in the fireplace, and overflowing with gratitude for the latest addition, our precious grandson. And there was no end to the blending in sight if you counted the four-legged critter I had adopted from the woods, the chickens in the coop, and whatever or whoever showed up. As Christmas drew close, I also experienced something I hadn't in years: I was completely pain-free. I slept through the night and was able to walk and jump lightly on a mini trampoline.

The change was not lost on Tim, who came home one afternoon and said, "I have your Christmas present in the car. It's too big to wrap up. Do you want it now?"

"Are you crazy?" I said. "Of course I want it now."

He escorted me out to the car and opened the hatchback. Inside were three large boxes. I recognized what it was immediately. A drum kit!

"Holy crap," I exclaimed.

True to form, as our household's official assembler of things, I put the kit together. The classic Ludwig set had six drums and three Zildjian cymbals, and hardware whose bright shine was outdone only by my smile. Once I finished each component, Tim carried it upstairs to the loft, which we had turned into a music room with his guitars and a freestanding keyboard. After the kit was fully assembled, I climbed up there, grabbed my sticks, and started whaling. I hadn't played in ages, but it felt great.

We kept Christmas simple. For dinner, we stuck to the tried and true: turkey and gravy, mashed potatoes, old-fashioned white-bread stuffing, a green bean casserole, and cranberry sauce. For dessert, I made a brown butter rosemary apple pie, a dish that I had wanted to try since I worked on the movie *Hometown Christmas* in 2018 and had a scene where my character invited her man-friend inside for a slice of rosemary apple pie. Two and a half years later, I finally made one, and it was stupid good.

Besides eating delicious food, there was nonstop game-playing straight through New Year's Eve. If we had been crazed drinkers, we would have been obliterated. Instead, we were consumed by cut-throat Uno and Yahtzee games. All three of us are competitive, but fortunately not with each other. So I remember our laughter more than I do who won. We also read. We played in the snow. We went sledding. We made snow angels. Afterward, we warmed up with hot cider. I painted and knitted. Despite being separated from so much family, I was content and in a good, upbeat mood—and I knew why.

Brown Butter Rosemary Apple Pie

3 pounds tart apples
1 tablespoon fresh lemon
  juice
1 teaspoon lemon zest—choose
  an organic lemon, since
  you're consuming the skin
¼ cup all-purpose flour
¼ cup packed light brown
  sugar
¼ cup organic granulated
  cane sugar
1 teaspoon kosher salt
½ teaspoon freshly ground
  nutmeg

½ teaspoon freshly grated
  cinnamon
2 teaspoons minced fresh
  rosemary leaves
4 tablespoons butter
1 egg, lightly beaten, for
  brushing
Demerara sugar, for sprinkling
1 box Pillsbury Pie Crusts (as
  with the sourdough bread, I
  am a failure at pie crust from
  scratch; this is the next best
  thing)
Crème fraîche, whipped cream,
  or ice cream, for serving

Peel, core, and cut the apples into wedges and place in a large bowl. Add the lemon juice and mix together to prevent the apples from browning. Add the zest, flour, brown sugar, cane sugar, salt, nutmeg, cinnamon, and rosemary, and stir to combine. Set aside while you make the brown butter.

In a light-colored sauté pan—so you can monitor the change in color as the butter browns—melt the butter over medium heat. Let it foam, and give it a swirl every so often to ensure it is cooking evenly. The process should take about 7 minutes; pay attention to the milk solids that settle at the bottom of the pan, as you don't want them to burn. Once the nutty aroma becomes apparent and the butter has turned a caramelly color, remove the pan from the heat.

Pour the brown butter and solids over the apple mixture and stir to combine. (If the milk solids are burned, you may choose not to add them—once the butter is cool enough to taste, try a little bit and see if you like the flavor, and then decide.) Cover and refrigerate the mixture at least 4 hours and up to overnight.

Drain the butter mixture from the apples into a saucepan and simmer until reduced by half. Add the reduced syrup back to the apple mixture and stir to combine. (Reducing the liquid will create a sumptuous pie rather than a watery one.)

Preheat the oven according to the directions on the pie crust box for a two-crust pie. Fill the bottom crust with the apple mixture. Cover with the top crust and crimp according to the directions on the pie crust box. Brush the top crust with the egg and sprinkle with Demerara sugar, and bake according to the directions on the pie crust box for a two-crust pie.

Cool completely on a wire rack and serve with crème fraîche, whipped cream, or ice cream.

I felt hopeful again. I loved changing the calendar to 2021, and as I did, I remembered some of the hilarious (and true) jokes about 2020 ("He chewed too loud" became the number one cause of divorce). Good riddance, 2020. We had a new president and a new administration coming into office. President Biden was going to be surrounded by capable people. He promised diversity. He was addressing problems, not causing them. He had policies. Talk of a vaccine's becoming available to all sounded real. I was comfortable with the way life had been stripped down and issues bared. Without honesty, there was no moving forward. Half the country was pressing for change and eager to right wrongs and prep for a better future. The other half was in denial.

It reminded me of therapy, of couple's therapy, where both sides agree to talk through their differences.

I was really leaning into this idea of needs versus wants. All that mattered to me was the safety and health of my loved ones, those with me, near me, and across the country. Hundreds of thousands of people in just the United States were dead. Never had Laura Ingalls Wilder's message about the "sweet, simple things of life" being the most real and important things resonated like it did then, as I looked ahead and wished Tim and Michael a happy New Year. I was so grateful for the sweet, simple things I saw every day, the sweetest being the love I felt for my family and friends. How did we go about making that a priority?

I remember that first weekend in January feeling significant. On Saturday, I cleaned the path to the chicken coop with the snowblower, which was hard but satisfying. Inside the coop, our new heated water holder was keeping the chickens' water from freezing. (I had come out one day and found them pecking at a frozen bowl.) The chickens were fine on their roosts; they hated the snow. On my way back to the house, I spotted raccoon tracks around the garden fence. Points to them for trying, but we had cleared and mulched the beds months earlier. Just after I made myself a mug of hot tea, Tim came back from town with news. He had seen Little with a larger deer he guessed was her mom and a few others down the road.

"They weren't *in* the road?" I said, alarmed and sounding very motherlike.

"No, they were frolicking," he said. "They were being deer."

"That's good," I said. "That must mean she's getting stronger."

Sunday began with the usual chicken chores, which was a challenge in temperatures that were well below freezing. Even bundled up, I bounced up and down and clapped my hands to keep warm. However, the frigid air set the stage for what turned out to be a spiritual sort of day—spiritual in the sense that everything quieted down and stilled until it felt like our immediate world had stopped. The critters we had grown accustomed to seeing—the groundhogs and chipmunks, the rabbits and raccoons, and even the deer—had vanished. Birds took the day off. I heard no tweets or chirps. At night, snow started to fall. I could hear it in the quiet, the sound of angels dancing. As a cold sleeper, I opened the window and was a happy girl.

"Seventeen degrees," I said to Tim. "We're going to sleep well."

"We're good," he said.

"I believe we are," I said. "This winter feels like a giant reset button."

"I hope."

"I think we're going to be okay. I think we're going to be able to start over and fix this mess."

"There's still a lot of people who believe the crazy."

"I just want to eat and cook and be with our family and play games and enjoy the stillness and the reset button."

On Monday, we woke up to a snow-covered winter wonderland. It was so beautiful. I felt so blessed. Later in the day I checked in with my friend Sandy, who still had her hands full. Before hanging up, we reminded each other that life was like a pearl necklace. A good one will have a knot on either side of each pearl so the pearls will not fall off if the string breaks. Sandy and I, in our experiences facing challenges, say that the gifts in our lives are the pearls and the hardships the knots. Without the knots, the pearls will slip away.

Two days later, I was savoring my pearls. I spent the late morning snuggled into the large easy chair in the living room. I was in my PJs, my knitting piled up in my lap. I looked down at my sock-covered feet and laughed.

"What's so funny?" Tim asked from the kitchen, where he was writing.

"Me," I said.

"You?"

"Yes. I have officially gone from a red-haired ingénue wearing designer clothes and riding in limousines and letting people walk all over me to a gray-haired granny on a recliner, contentedly knitting while wearing socks, and putting up with zero BS and giving even fewer fucks."

"It suits you."

"It does."

"It's sexy."

"You know it."

I had the news on the TV in the background but I wasn't paying attention to coverage of the outgoing president spewing his lies about the lost election to his brainwashed brethren. I was waiting for the day's more significant event: the House's voting to certify the results of the Electoral College. Though confident it would happen, I was curious to see what kind of shenanigans the biggest toadies would pull. I knew they would do something. But I didn't expect the news alert that came across my phone. The Capitol was on lockdown.

WTF?

I hollered to Tim and texted Michael in the trailer to come and watch with me. For the rest of the afternoon, we watched the slow encroachment of mobs massing in front of the United States Capitol and then, as seemed inevitable, breaking past police and locked doors and storming inside, until they had sent House and Senate members and Vice President Pence and his family fleeing for their safety. I had been in that building many times. I kept waiting for the police to stop it. When they failed, I assumed the National Guard would come in. We had seen them at every other protest over the summer.

We had seen them tear-gas peaceful protestors in front of St. John's Church last June. As far as I was concerned, that embodied the total insanity into which that administration had descended.

That is, until now. I texted friends I suspected might be there and potentially in danger, ABC news correspondent Gloria Riviera and US representatives Debbie Dingell and Cheri Bustos. I didn't hear back from anyone. Hours later, Gloria let me know she was on the other side of the country and her kids and husband, Jim, were fine. Horrified but fine. Tim and I held hands. As the violence got worse, I cried. The visuals were absolutely horrendous. Was this the end result of the outgoing guy's leadership? Four years earlier, he had spoken about "American carnage." Now we were seeing it manifested like some bizarre Nostradamus prophecy.

"I feel like America has gone insane," I said.

"Like we're having a nervous breakdown," Michael said.

"More like multiple personality disorder," I said.

Two weeks later, I was curled up in the same chair, with Tim and Michael, watching the inauguration in an entirely different frame of mind. I hadn't really paid attention to inaugurations previously. I thought this one was beautiful and inspiring. I teared up when I witnessed the historically significant moment Kamala Harris was sworn in. I felt relief seeing Joe and Jill Biden together. And I cheered when I saw Joe get out of his car and walk down Pennsylvania Avenue. I remembered back to when I was running for president of the Screen Actors Guild. One day shortly after the September 11 terrorist attacks, I was supposed to fly to New York for a fundraiser. Too afraid to board a plane, I canceled the event, prompting my running mate, actor Mike Farrell, a clear thinker and steady presence, to remind me that the objective of the terrorism was to terrify me and all the rest of us into not living our lives to the fullest.

I was thinking about that as I watched Joe waving to the crowd. I thought, If Grandpa's going to do that and Grandma isn't yanking him back into the car, then I'm good. I knew it was meant to convey a message, and I got it. I felt safe. I felt hopeful. I felt hope returning. Hope was oxygen for the soul. I reached for the new seed catalog that had recently arrived in the mail. I had tossed it on a nearby table. Now, with strains of Joni Mitchell playing in my head, it was time to get back to the garden, time to start planning our garden again.

Back to the Garden

There were perfect cheese soufflés. There was finger-lickin'-good fried chicken. There were drives out to the Laundrette. There were movie nights, music afternoons, and days when we improvised ideas and made each other laugh. We wrote. We pitched ideas. We Zoomed. I knitted my first baby sweater and hat. My COVID nineteen was actually twenty-five, and after getting clearance from Dr. Bray, I found my Cardio Barre DVD and worked out. I stretched, flexed, twisted, and took two Advil.

This was life when it was five degrees outside chez Gilbert-Busfield. We bided our time through the wintery, overcast skies and blustery cold, waiting for spring and, most important, for our turn to get vaccinated.

My mother was vaccinated in February, a privilege and a precaution due to her age. Seeing her on Zoom, though, she was ageless. But this first vaccine was a big deal for our family. It was our own modern *Little House* adventure. She was leading us down the treacherous path; we were holding each other's hands as we followed her toward safety. Our family chat was full of hearts and exclamation points. My mother was starving for the opportunity to hug grandchildren again.

At fifty-seven, I missed my mom. I missed my children. I wanted to hug my grandchildren and make sure I met the new one on the way. Both the news and the mounting anticipation of when we might qualify for our own vaccines highlighted everything we had reconfirmed was most important and essential to our happiness, which was family and health, followed by all the pleasures and annoyances that came with them—and then of course work and paying for all the things that complicated modern life.

But God, what was life without being able to hug your mom and your kids? That was the question, the emotional thread that connected all of us, everywhere, and especially women, who could empathize as mothers and daughters with other mothers and daughters, whether we were talking about COVID, shootings, injustice, hunger, the displacement of refugees, or any of the myriad other crises wherein we saw mothers holding babies or crying over children with wide, pleading eyes.

I know this may sound like a leap, but those sentiments were why I loved putting my hands in the dirt and craved the arrival of spring, when Tim and I would turn over the soil, replenish it with compost, and plant our veggies. It felt good. It smelled good. It also felt good to laze around in my flannel PJs and knit while Josephine napped (and snored) against my outstretched legs.

By early March, vaccines were being given to essential workers and those sixty-five and older. Though we were eager to get our jabs, Tim and I weren't sure when shots would be available to us.

We knew the criteria were going to change and expand to get more people vaccinated, but we had no choice except to wait. We heard about people showing up at places where vaccines were being given and waiting to see if there were leftovers at the end of the day. We had friends who tried that route with varying success. Then I read that people working at vaccination centers, including volunteers, were given a shot if there were leftovers, so we signed up to work at our local clinic in Sullivan County.

After our applications were approved, we attended the next volunteer event. They were looking for people who could type fast. I wasn't one of those people. But Tim was an expert typist, and he spent the next day setting up second-shot appointments for the nearly six hundred people who got vaccinated during his shift. Toward the end of his workday, they offered him a leftover Johnson & Johnson vaccine. He gladly took it. One and done. He asked if there was a chance they might also have an extra shot for his wife. One of the nurses said she would let him know at the end of the day.

Hours later, Tim called. I was in the car with Michael, heading into Barryville. I told him that I was an hour away.

"She's an hour away," I heard him tell the nurse.

"If she can get here by then, because we close in an hour, we will have a shot for her," she said.

"Did you hear that?" Tim asked me.

"I'm already standing on the accelerator," I said.

We pulled in just under the deadline and Tim whisked me inside. As I waited, Tim was just starting to get chills in reaction to his J & J vaccine. I asked the nurse if they had a third extra dose for my son. When she said no, Tim and Michael got in the car and started home, and I received my shot. While I was waiting my fifteen minutes afterward, the nurse asked how far away my son was; the person with the last appointment of the day had just called and canceled. I called the guys, they made a sudden bat-turn, and Michael received the last shot of the day.

"Good jab, everyone," I said.

Once we got home, I saw Tim was fading fast. A few years before, he'd had rotator cuff surgery—which I'd had as well and considered one of the most painful surgeries in my life—and I still hadn't been able to get him to slow down. But the J & J shot took a toll. I knew he must have been suffering badly, and he was. He looked at me and said, "I have to go to bed," and he barely woke up for the next eighteen hours.

Michael and I had Moderna vaccines, and our arms were hella sore, but that was it. Actually, that's not quite accurate. I got very emotional. I had an intense desire to hug my kids, my grandkids, my mother, my sister, my nieces and nephews, and my friends who had also been vaccinated. Four weeks later, I returned for my second shot and also volunteered, walking people through their second dose. I shared many tears of relief, smizes, and even some hugs. It was so nice to be in a room filled with hope, compassion, and joy.

And it wasn't just us humans who felt that way. At the end of my shift, I got kisses and snuggles from a lovely dog being trained as a service dog for the blind.

I understood stories I had read about how people scooped up their kids off playgrounds and rushed them to get the polio vaccine when it became available in 1955. Like, duh, why wouldn't you? I related to the joy virtuoso cellist Yo-Yo Ma felt when he gave an impromptu concert in the parking lot of the place where he got vaccinated in the Berkshires. And I nodded when I heard that after ninety-five-year-old Dick Van Dyke got his vaccination, he led those around him in a chorus of "A Spoonful of Sugar."

Yes! I thought we should all be singing and dancing. COVID wasn't going to kill those of us who had been vaccinated, and we were going to be able to open stores and theaters and concert venues and travel.

On our group text, I informed my mom and sister that Tim and I were vaccinated and already planning a cross-country road trip for summer and would be in LA in mid-June. *You can stay here*, my mom immediately replied. Then Sara texted back that we could stay with her, too. The conversation almost gave me whiplash. It was so oddly and suddenly and delightfully ordinary. I wouldn't say normal, because nothing was normal yet and it might not ever be. But the conversations dressed in familiar clothes.

Others followed. As more friends became vaccinated, we asked each other, "Have you had one or two? Two? Great, when are we getting together for dinner?"

One day Tim and I were in the city and we did something we hadn't done in ages. We went to a movie. In a movie theater. Michael joined us at the last minute and we comprised three of the nine people in the theater, which probably had room for six hundred. We all were so socially distanced it felt antisocial. But it was a weekday matinee. In the midst of a pandemic. And the film was *Tenet*, which no one understood anyway, including me. So we were not concerned about a fight for seats.

Not that it mattered. I carried my mix of hot buttered popcorn and Sour Patch Kids into the theater as if I was carrying two Emmy Awards and placed kernel after kernel and kid after kid under my mask while sitting next to my hubby, a tiny but fantastic reminder of why I love going to the movies.

As much as we loved the city, Tim and I were happiest when we were at the Cabbage. We talked about this often; it was one of the effects of the lockdown. When we first moved out to the country, we spent all of our time in the city and this little cottage was supposed to be our escape. But it had flipped. Maybe we had, too. We wanted to spend all of our time in the country and treat the city as an escape, a place for work, a nice dinner, a chance to see the best theater in the world, and then see ya later.

I began to regard our apartment as a nice hotel suite; ordering from DoorDash was like having room service delivered. In the same way I made no apologies for replenishing my supply of La Mer face cream, I was not against treating myself or ourselves to some small indulgences from time to time. But that's not who either of us were. The lure of the Cabbage was proof that there was no going back to normal. We were working through the pandemic, marching toward the light and whatever it was illuminating. It could have been worse; it could have been better. The only sure bet was that life was going to be different.

I believed that was a good thing. As novelist Thomas Wolfe wrote in *You Can't Go Home Again*, "Make your mistakes, take your chances, look silly, but keep on going." We were, enthusiastically. Tim and I mapped out a slew of projects that would carry us through the summer. We planned to tear down the old ramshackle shed and order two additional shipping containers to complement the two we already had. We wanted to put them together, fashion windows and doors, and eventually side them with planks cut from trees on our property. We began to enlarge the garden. And we worked at finding creative ways to cook eggs.

Only once did we have so many eggs that I gave a dozen to a neighbor. Otherwise we kept up with the girls, who worked very hard for us and rarely if ever disappointed. I made a lot of frittatas through the spring. We also ate them hard-boiled, scrambled, soft-boiled, sunny-side up, over easy, ranchero style, and poached. We ate enough that our doctor, following our annual physicals, suggested that we might want to join a gym and get more exercise.

I suppose that was a polite way of saying, "You guys are clearly enjoying the fat of the land, and eating it, too, but please, watch your cholesterol." Like everyone else, we were working to strike a before-and-after balance. We had no answers to questions, only a gut feeling—well, that and a new plant-based diet.

"It's about how to continue in this new reality without losing sight of all the things we've learned," I said to Tim one night after dinner. "Needs versus wants. Making things simpler and less complicated and being more self-reliant."

"Being mindful," Tim said. "Taking care of ourselves to the best of our ability."

"Yes, everyone is healing." I nodded. "We have to try not to get caught up in the craziness again—the craziness of having too many things, of being spread too thin, of overspending and overdoing."

"For us, at least, things have gotten pretty simple."

"And it's so much easier to live this way."

I was all for simplicity, no matter what it meant I had to tackle on my own. The carpet needed cleaning? No problem. I rented a carpet cleaner and washed our carpets. Plumbing issues? Ditto. I canceled an appointment in the city one day, and the reason made me laugh as I said it: "We are having the cesspool sucked out today and I have to be here." This was my little house on the prairie.

Then, just like that, it was spring again. Grass was growing, birds were singing, trees were in bloom. I picked a giant handful of forsythia and stuck it in a vase in the corner of our bedroom. The branches were long, some over four feet, and loaded with bright yellow flowers that set the room ablaze with color. One look left no doubt that winter was over. Nature's neon sign clearly declared the outdoors back and open for business.

On Earth Day, I tacked a picture of our planet on the fridge and wrote, "Love Your Mother." My old hippie flag was flying proudly. Tim and I celebrated our eighth wedding anniversary. Both of us agreed it just kept getting better.

Sort of. We offered to dog-sit our grandpup, Ducky, a wheaten terrier, while his mom and dad (Tim's son Willy) went on a short vacation. Ducky, who lived in the city, was in paradise on our fourteen acres, running around, chasing animals, exploring, and playing ball. He was also eating tons of deer and rabbit poop, which upset his intestines and turned our little visit into a festival of explosive puppy diarrhea. Having dealt with numerous dogs in the past, we were unfazed. We took him off food for thirty-six hours; put him on pumpkin, rice, and goat's milk; and walked him on a leash. I also reserved the carpet cleaner again for after Ducky went back to the city.

In mid-April, our seeds arrived. After months of back-and-forth ("What kind of lettuce do you hate? Because I'm going to plant lettuce. So if there's something you don't want . . ."), we had decided on buttercrunch lettuce, more green beans, Napa cabbage, Roma tomatoes (Tim's favorite), heirloom tomatoes, Walla Walla onions, garlic, bok choy, zucchini, grapes, and watermelon. We had also ordered a bunch of returnees from the previous year: parsley, oregano, basil, thyme, rosemary, cilantro, sunflowers, snapdragons, zinnias, cosmos, petunias, pansies, amaranth, feverfew, dahlias, fuchsias, and bishop's weed.

On May 2, we finished planting and I announced to Tim and Josephine and all the critters watching us from their branches and posts in the woods that the garden was officially started. In case our furry and feathered friends didn't understand the rules, I added that nothing was to be eaten or tasted or dug up until it was ready.

"Timmy, we smell . . . as Margaret Atwood said, the way one should smell in the spring," I said.

"And how's that?" he asked. "Like dirt?"

"Yup."

"And sweat?"

"Yup."

"And fertilizer?"

"You betcha."

"And sunscreen?"

"I don't know that she said that, but maybe, if she's translucent like us." I laughed.

It was a sweet and satisfying moment. We were back in our

garden, and I sensed that Tim and I were both exactly where we should be.

Even without the pandemic, I think Tim and I would have found ourselves in this spot. Both of us were headed in this direction regardless. The blessing was that we met at the right time in our lives and took this journey together, as a couple, and as we got deeper into the lifestyle, we recognized that this was who we wanted to be. And we had this life with each other. I remember watching the movie *Legends of the Fall*, an epic drama about a father and his sons living in the wilderness. After all this trauma and drama, Brad Pitt's character returns home to his ailing father (Anthony Hopkins) and marries a young woman who is the daughter of the caretakers of the property. They have two babies. And the narrator says that he has come into the quiet heart of his life. That's the thing I keep thinking about. I have come into the quiet heart of my life. I love to work. I love acting. I love what I do. But I don't have the hunger I did in my twenties and thirties. I don't have the same ambition. My career is a part of who I am. But not all of who I am. Not the be-all, end-all it was when I was younger. And that is such a comfort. To know that. To know that I am so much more.

On May 8, a few days after we finished planting the garden, and after the need for Advil had passed, I turned fifty-seven years old. I had a spectacular day of doing nothing. I cut flowers and brought them into the house. I announced that spring was in the house. As was the birthday girl. I snapped a selfie and—surprise, surprise— really liked the way I looked. In jammies, sitting in a recliner. No makeup, no filter. This is me, I thought, finally happy in my own skin. No fillers or Botox, no implants, no hair color. Just me. This is happy. This is healthy. This is strong. This is rooted. This is confident. This is a woman who has earned her opinions. This is quiet, still, and at peace . . . finally.

Yes, my joints are a bit stiffer and I don't have the physical strength I once had. But I look at those things as some of the gifts of aging. They force me to slow down and be more mindful and appreciative of the little things, along with my connections to other people and this place. They remind me that life is not always easy, not for any of us, but I would rather be here than the alternative. It is a joy to watch my children and their children grow and learn and develop into loving human beings. It is also a blessing to be loved and cherished by such an extraordinary man and to have a true and eternal partnership. How blessed I am to have all these gifts.

This is the takeaway from the past year and a half.

This is what I want to keep with me going forward.

How blessed we are to be here and be healthy.

How blessed we are to have these extraordinary gifts.

How blessed we are to have and to help each other.

How blessed we are to have been able to make a living doing what we love.

How blessed we are to be surrounded by our big, beautiful family.

How blessed we are to have the love and support of our incredible circle of friends.

How blessed we are to have a roof over our heads and food to eat.

How blessed we are to live in this beautifully imperfect country.

How blessed we are to have the mutual respect, understanding, love, and laughter that are the foundations of our marriage.

How blessed we are that spring is in the house.

How blessed we are to live in this cozy home that we have created together.

How blessed we are to live the dream.

The dream we never even knew we had until we dared to live it.

Afterword
Ripley—Believe It or Not

All you need is love, love
Love is all you need.
JOHN LENNON AND PAUL McCARTNEY

It was a scary couple of weeks. In late April, I had my annual mammogram and ultrasound. I left my doctor's office having been told everything was fine—but when I got back to our apartment about twenty minutes later, there was a voicemail message from my doctor, asking me to call the office or his cell phone, which he then recited, ASAP. It turned out he had compared that day's mammogram to last year's and noticed some calcifications. He asked me to return the next day for a more in-depth mammogram.

That led to a biopsy two weeks later. I did a little web research into what I might be dealing with, but I didn't dive too deep. I gathered enough information from Dr. Google to feel informed but not panic myself, which was the right decision—always the right decision—as the calcifications, to my great relief, turned out to be benign. In the meantime, I had put myself through the wringer. I jumped up and down, I cried, I hugged Tim, I kissed Josephine, I texted the few friends I had told, I did the same with my mother and sister, and then I stepped outside and basked in the sunshine.

In the days afterward, I enjoyed feeling relieved. I spoke to several women I knew who'd had similar experiences. Talking to them was therapeutic and helpful. They reinforced the idea that I was not alone, that we all are so much more alike than we know. We are also resilient and fragile at the same time, and it's vital to recognize this and support each other through the ups and downs with understanding and kindness.

Relief inspired me to rant about the privilege of good health care. I didn't care who I bored or bothered. I wanted to make a difference—and I did in my own unexpected way. A few days after getting the all-clear signal from my doctor, Tim and I were driving back to the Cabbage after working out. I was behind the wheel, and I saw something ahead of us in the road.

"What's that—a dog?" I said. "Uh-oh, that's not good."

As we got closer, I realized it wasn't a dog. It was a teeny tiny baby deer. She was almost the size of Josephine but with slightly longer legs. I glanced in the rearview mirror and saw several cars behind us. Another couple were headed up the road on the other side. I stopped our car, jumped out, and stood in the middle of the road with my hands up like a traffic cop, bringing drivers on both sides to a halt. I gestured "Thank you" to them.

As I did this, Baby Doe walked toward me. Hers was barely a walk. It was more like a shaky, tentative toddle.

"Hello, little one," I cooed.

I held out my arms and made myself open and safe. Then I noticed the mama deer was up the embankment on the other side of the road. The baby deer didn't want me. She wanted her mother. But I saw she was slipping on the asphalt, unsure of her footing, as newborns are. I was now assuming she was that young, a very new arrival. So instead of picking her up, I sort of corralled the scared little thing and nudged her off the road and up the hill toward her mom. The whole time the other cars remained stopped, and after I helped the baby deer to safety, I returned to my car, pausing in the middle of the road to take a bow and thank everyone. Several drivers honked their horns in appreciation. Tim was sitting in our vehicle, applauding.

"Bravo."

It was a perfect Halfpint-y day.

And not the only one. One day I turned out of our driveway and the tiniest baby bear ran across the road in front of me. I did not get out of the car to make sure it was okay because when there's a baby bear, there is always a mama bear nearby. Then another little friend stopped by to visit. An ovenbird, a member of the warbler family, sat on our deck one morning as if she had stopped by to chat. I thought she might be hurt, so I gave her some water and sat down next to her. She let me pick her up and hold her for about twenty minutes. We talked. She was in no hurry to get away. Then we were done. She cocked her head to look at me and say goodbye before flying back into the woods. It was odd and wonderful and another reminder that we are not alone. We all are in this together, including our fine feathered friends.

Indeed, a short time later, our kitchen turned into a chicken clinic. I noticed Little Miss Cotton had a bare spot on her back where the other hens had pecked at it. This was what it meant to be henpecked. I brought her inside, where Tim and I gave her lots of TLC until she healed. Until then, I didn't know chickens were cannibals. They liked to pull at new pin feathers to get at a tiny vein in them. It gets bloody and drives them into a picking and pecking frenzy. The blood is yummy to them—and disgusting to me.

By early June, Dakota and Marissa were about to welcome their first child into this world. From their home in Austin, they let me know everything was good and the mama-to-be was feeling healthy and ready. Dakota was nervous and excited. In other words, he was a normal first-time father. I did not pretend anything about becoming a grandmother again was normal. It was a miracle. And I warned that anyone not into babies was soon going to find me very boring.

I wasn't the only one with grandparent fever—vaccinated and masked, Tim flew to Sacramento and got in some important and long-overdue grandpa time with his daughter's children, Ruby and Eli. As he made his way back to Highland Lake, I kept tabs on Marissa and Dakota. I was relieved they were on schedule because Tim and I had a short work trip to Pittsburgh that we didn't want to cancel. We arranged to visit them a week or so after they brought the baby home. Pandemic or not, my calendar was full. All I had to figure out was a convenient way to travel with Josephine. My aging beauty was not as nimble as she had been in years past.

But she looked up at me from where she was nuzzled against my leg, seeming to assure me that she wouldn't be a problem. "I know," I told her. "I love you, too."

Then it was baby time. In the wee hours of June 8, Marissa's water broke. Already days late, she was thrilled—and ready. Dakota drove her to the hospital and sure enough, she was already in labor. He texted updates throughout the whole process. She was calm and resting easily, he said. Everything proceeding according to the book, he added later. By afternoon, she was in intense labor. She got an epidural. A couple of hours later, Dakota texted that he had to go. "She's starting the pushing part."

I was broadcasting all this information in real time to my mother and sister on a group text, and when the flow of information stopped and I didn't hear anything from Dakota for several hours, it set off a chain of frustrated reactions among us: *What the hell? Where is she? How much does she weigh? What does she look like? Where are the pictures?* I explained that they were probably surrounded by doctors and nurses who were likely inundating them with information and, not to mention, getting to know their daughter, which my mother and sister understood and respected, as did I. But we still wanted to know what the hell was going on.

Finally, a picture of Ripley Lou Brinkman arrived, followed by another picture, and all was forgiven. Weighing seven pounds, seven ounces, and measuring nineteen and a half inches, she arrived at 6:18 p.m. Central time and was pink, beautiful, and perfect. Tim and I were the happiest nana and papa on the planet. Over the next hour, the entire family checked in. All of us celebrated the newest member of the family.

It was close to eight o'clock. The sun was setting, and the sky was changing from dusk to night. Tim gave Josephine dinner, let her out, and handed her a cookie after she came back in, as we always did. The two of us also had dinner, rehashed all the excitement, looked at baby pictures on our phone, counted our blessings, and finally, as the day wound down, we got ready for bed.

I went into the bathroom to wash my face. In the midst of that, I stepped back into the bedroom to grab something, and when I came out, I saw Josephine lying in the middle of the living room floor. It looked like she had fallen asleep there. Just laid down for a snooze. But I saw her leg was bent kind of funny. On closer inspection, I saw she had also pooped. That didn't look right.

"Josie," I called out. "Jose! Josephine!"

She didn't respond. Nothing. I glanced at Tim, who had walked into the room, and said, "Timmy . . . oh no, oh no, oh no." He turned the light on, and I knew immediately that she was dead. Lying that way, making a mess—that wasn't her style. Seeing no evidence of trauma, I assumed that her heart had stopped midstep and she had gone. I lost it, and dropped to my knees weeping and repeating, "Oh no, oh no, oh no . . . ," over and over.

A few moments later I gathered myself and tucked her little foot under her and made sure she was comfortable. I whispered into her ear that I loved her and told her what a good, sweet, special dog she was. And I told her to go to Baba. Tim kneeled beside us and whispered his goodbyes to her, and then we just sat with her for a spell. After a while, I called the vet, told him what had happened, and said I didn't know what to do.

"I've had dogs die in the yard," I said. "I've had them put down. But I've never had a dog just walk into the room and drop dead."

We wrapped her in a blanket, put her in a crate, and set her in the air-conditioned trailer, where she would not get hot in the humid summer air. I kept going outside to check on her. I was so in denial, speeding through all five stages of grief that night. My heart had whiplash after having experienced such joy earlier in the evening. On my way out to check on her at one point, I turned to Tim and said, "I keep thinking she's sitting up in there, wondering why she's in there without us, and when I go in, she'll say, 'Where were you guys?'"

But she was gone. Her passing came just two hours after Ripley was born. It was a true believe-it-or-not moment. It was as peaceful as it was sudden. She simply stopped. We are sure she was making room and making it easier for us to travel and see our kids and grandkids. This good, sweet dog had an amazing life and touched many people, from my coworkers to children in hospitals and so many others in between. Most important, she was loved—beloved, even—and she knew it.

And I knew I was so lucky to be the recipient of her unconditional and unlimited reservoir of love. *Goodbye, my sweet Josie, Joser, Joseph, Jeebs. I love you.*

Two weeks later, I was sitting on a large red sofa and holding Ripley Lou in my arms. I watched her eyes flutter. After she burped, the most beautiful, fragile, perfectly formed smile appeared on her tiny pink lips. I swaddled her in a blanket and let her nestle into my chest, and soon she was asleep. I couldn't have been happier. To me, this was bliss. A sleeping newborn in my arms. My granddaughter. My heart. My beloved one.

This is where I should end. But I must share one more thing. Because the next day Timmy, who had stayed behind to oversee some new work at the Cabbage, texted me a video of a baby deer frolicking in our backyard under the watchful eye of her mother.

Was it the baby deer I had rescued from traffic the previous month? I hoped. She looked familiar. A great big smile appeared on my face as I watched her run. This was the circle of life—and I was in the center of it.

I had arrived in it the same and only way any of us do: by following my heart.

I hope that more and more people see that's the best thing we can do for each other as we travel into the future together. Be kind and follow our hearts.

Now put this book down, cue the Beatles song, turn it up real loud, and sing: *Love, love, love* . . .

Nana out.

Acknowledgments

Books do not write themselves. It took several villages of talented people to get this book into your hands, dear reader. Thank goodness for Zoom, email, cell phones, Instagram, and carrier pigeon.

First, I must acknowledge my team at Simon & Schuster's Gallery Books. From the start, this project was a labor of love, and I will forever be grateful to Jen Bergstrom, Lauren Spiegel, Taylor Rondestvedt, and everyone else at Gallery who worked with them to nurture this adventure that I took with my husband into a book. Thank you for always encouraging me to write what I felt in my heart.

Thank you, thank you, a million times to my secret weapon and most excellent pal Todd Gold. Todd, there are so many more stories for us to tell. I can't wait for the next one.

To my literary agent, Dan Strone at the Trident Media Group, who, in 2020, saw me being interviewed by Mo Rocca on *CBS This*

Morning and then called me and said, "I think there's a book here." Thank you, Dan.

Thank you, thank you, Brian Bowen Smith and Shea Bowen-Smith for your warm, embracing friendship and for the beautiful image that graces the cover of this book.

To Michelle Coursey, makeup and hair artist extraordinaire. From talk shows to print to this book's cover, you've helped me to feel confident and comfortable in my own skin. Here's to more fun evenings with you, Matt, and Lady Cookie hanging out at the Cabbage and playing Cards Against Humanity.

I must also thank my team at Innovative Artists, Jonathan Howard, Nevin Dolcefino, Gary Gersh, Chris Stego, Brian Davidson, and Lisa Lieberman, for always keeping the faith and helping me to proclaim myself still a working actor fifty-five years after my very first job.

As always, immense love and gratitude to my dear, stalwart friend and publicist, Ame Van Iden. Our decades-long working relationship has been one of the great highlights of my career. Our friendship is a treasure that never ceases to lift my spirits. Now, as one farm girl to another, thank you.

I owe so much gratitude to Michael Landon and my entire *Little House* family. Every day I recall something I learned from one of you all those years ago. Thank you all for helping me to become the woman I am today.

To my wonderful friends in the Catskills, Johnny and Roswell; Dan, Fawn, and Savannah Schneider and the rest of the Schneider family; Sal; E; Michelle; and everyone there who welcomed us with open arms.

A lifetime of gratitude to Dr. Robert Bray, his entire staff, and his wonderful family. Your impact on my life is truly immeasurable. Because of all of you, I am one hundred percent pain-free for the first time in decades.

Thank you, thank you to Alex Finch and Carrie Nydeck-Finch for helping to make our house a home. Your friendship is one of the greatest gifts Tim has shared with me. I love you guys!!

To my dear girlfriends, led by the incomparable Sandy Peckinpah. What would we have done without one another all these years? Know that just as you are always there for me, I am always there for you. I love you, ladies and my dearest BFF.

My sweet sister, Sara, you have been someone I've crowed about since the moment you were born. But seeing you now, a show business mogul, mother, creator, and force to be reckoned with, well, my heart just explodes with pride and love. Despite all of your tremendous accomplishments, you will always be the sweet little baby I used to tickle with my pigtails.

To my four boys . . . scratch that . . . four men, Sam, Lee, Dakota, and Michael. When I think of you, I think of a quote from *The Miracle Worker*: "You'll learn, we don't just keep our children safe. They keep us safe." That's especially true now that you are all so much taller than me. I love you each so much. You guys have made my life so much richer than I could have imagined. Your love for one another should be a lesson to any blended family. I am so very proud of the men you have become.

My darling daughters-in-law, Andrea and Marissa. Boy, did I hit the in-law lottery with you two. You truly are the daughters I never had. How blessed I am that my boys found you and you said, "Yes." I love you!!!

To Willy, Daisy, and Sam for teaching me such unexpected and necessary lessons. Thank you also to Daisy and Willy for giving your dad and me our beloved grandchildren, Vito, Aury, Bowen, Ruby, and Eli.

Timmy, I don't know that I can even find words to thank you for all you have brought into my life. This book could have started with "A man walks into a bar . . . ," but it's no joke. You are my beloved, and I hold your heart in my heart through this lifetime and onward into the next and the next and the next . . .

A most heartfelt thank-you to David Darlington and Kathy Wood for loving me enough to let me go.

Where would I be and who would I be were it not for Barbara and Paul Gilbert, the two who scooped up Baby Girl Darlington and made her Melissa Ellen Gilbert?

Daddy, I miss you every day. I honor you every day. I love you every day. I will always be your Miss Melissa-doo. See you next time, Daddy-Bear.

Finally, Mom, what a journey we have been on together. We have traveled all over the world, sometimes crawling down hotel hallways because we were laughing too hard to walk. Sure, we have had fierce conflicts. What mother and daughter don't? But more important, we share a fierce love for each other, the kind of love that overrides everything else. No matter how far away I have gone, physically or emotionally, you have always been there, waiting patiently for my return. I am so happy we are here now, at this glorious, peaceful, loving place. Watching you become a great-grandmother has been so incredibly moving for me. I thank God, Buddha, Allah, Zoroaster, Mohammed, Abraham, and Meher Baba for making sure you were the one who took me into your heart and into your home. I love you, my beautiful, delicate, talented, deeply funny, and impossibly glamorous mother and I always, always will. Xo, Your Wissey